THE HINDU PERSONALITY IN EDUCATION

The Hindu Personality in Education

Tagore • Gandhi • Aurobindo

WILLIAM CENKNER

MANOHAR
2025

First published 1976
Reprinted 1993, 2020, 2022, 2023, 2024

ISBN 978-93-90035-01-4

Published by
Ajay Kumar Jain *for*
Manohar Publishers & Distributors
4753/23 Ansari Road, Daryaganj
New Delhi 110 002

Printed at
Replika Press Pvt. Ltd.

Contents

To

Thomas Berry

Friend, Teacher, Guide

Introduction

One of the most challenging areas of Indian studies is the religious personality within contemporary Hinduism. Several philosophical works and cultural histories have demonstrated the vitality of the high religious personality in twentieth century Indian development. This particular study, however, arises out of a conviction that India has important things to say to the West and to the world not only in a theoretical way but also in a practical way. Educational reform is one of the most practical activities of man, drawing upon the full range of his thought and personality for articulation. It is difficult to grasp the significance of an extraordinary personality, for no simple phenomenological structure is universally applicable. Scholars have in the past approached the religious personality historically or even philosophically, but few studies have indicated how practical activity follows closely upon the character and thought of the figure. For a thorough understanding of such a personality, it is necessary to see how his entrance into the practical affairs of life, even secular activity, and in this case education, is intimately connected with his basic thought and the structure of his own personality.

One methodological problem in the study of the religious personality is to uncover the consistency between the individual and his thought and activity. The continuity between personality, philosophy and action should be rigorously consistent when one is dealing with a highly spiritual figure. Each of the three parts of this work begins with a brief consideration of the personality of the man under consideration, historically outlined around a dominating characteristic which has emerged from his individual life. The second step of investigation is a study of a single aspect of his philosophy, namely, his philosophy of man wherein the significant quality of his personality becomes the philosophical vision for an understanding of man. The major part of the study is an analysis of the practical activity which these three figures shared, that is, the development of an educational theory and praxis. It will be seen that their philosophy of man is inherent in their articulation of an educational theory. The process reveals that the three individuals under consideration were generally consistent in their self-understanding and in their articulation of the nature of man and the building of future humanity through education.

Most studies in contemporary Hinduism point to the role of the British in India along with Christian missionaries and the work of orientalists as stimulants to the Indian renaissance in the nineteenth and twentieth centuries. But as Sri Aurobindo has pointed out, the renaissance was governed primarily by the principle of interiority. Every creative period in Indian development, the Vedic period, the time of classical Sanskrit works, the age of *bhakti*, even medieval sectarianism, was a new experience of the spirit within human life. The principle of interiority operating within the Indian renaissance was a rediscovery of the spiritual within life which increased both the power and effectiveness of human life. The great personalities of recent Hinduism made this discovery in their own lives, in the lives of their people and the life of the nation, and hence were able to participate in the restoration of Indian life which ushered India into the modern period. Regardless of the impact of the processes of Sanskritization, secularization or Westernization, the spiritual man was both the spear-head and the source of the renaissance. He was able to bridge the gap between change and continuity, tradition and modernity. And even these processes are better understood in the lives of the extraordinary men and women of the period than in the more general terms of history and society.

Education is a practical activity, and it became for some of the leaders of contemporary Indian life the most practical and the most public activity they embraced. Indian education has been a controversial and disruptive issue from the time of the British presence in the nineteenth century to the present with the impact of still prevailing Western influences. By the turn of the century a million Indians had received a Western education either at home in missionary schools and public institutions which had aped Western forms or had gone abroad for education. By the end of the first quarter of the century women were eagerly taking to education in large numbers and this had a further impact on the direction of education in India. From the beginning of the independence movement, education was recognized as the means of building up the new nation to confront modernity and to establish roots in the cultural traditions of four thousand years. Rabindranath Tagore, Mohandas K. Gandhi and Sri Aurobindo saw education as the process through which national restoration could take place on a comprehensive scale if the principle of interiority, the discovery of the spiritual at the heart of life, were pursued.

These three figures have been selected because their value as religious personalities endures. Gandhi and Tagore are still widely read and since the 1972 centenary of Sri Aurobindo's birth, he has become a new discovery for many as recent editions of his writings and studies about him rapidly increase. They are not merely Indian personalities at this moment in history but world figures who will have greater significance in the future. Gandhi, of course, more than any single person in Indian history has been thoroughly and exhaustingly researched to such a degree that the weight of his personality and the wholeness of the man is easily lost. Few are aware of the more practical affairs of his life which were *āśram* life with his disciples and specific social reforms such as in the field of education. A little introduction has been given in the case of Tagore for an audience who know him mainly through the translations of some few poems, short stories and novels. Outside of India few know Tagore as the leading Asian educator of the first half of this century. In the case of Sri Aurobindo, education is a means whereby a neophyte could approach the richness and vastness of the man and his accomplishments.

These three men were in one sense primarily reformers for they looked at nothing of the past with indifference but built their experiences on the transformation of what had been given. So too in terms of education, they looked to the past but built an educational experience upon the transformation of that past. They were reformers in the most practical dimension of public life: education. Because they grasped how the spiritual had renewed every past golden age in India's history and were able to revive this perception and experience in a contemporary moment, they have significance for us today. They offer a challenge to us today, East and West, as we again enter a new age in both religion and education with the twenty-first century pressing upon us.

I express appreciation to the many individuals in India who were of assistance to me in my research during the summer of 1973. I would especially thank those who came to my aid at various centres: the Gandhi Memorial Museum and Library at the Rajghat, New Delhi; the National Library, Calcutta; Visva-Bharati University, Santiniketan, and especially the Director, Professor Santosh Chandra Sengupta, and the staff of the Centre of Advanced Study in Philosophy; the Gandhi *āśram* at Sevagram which I visited with Vinoba; to Professor Balasubramanian, Centre of Advanced Study in Philosophy, University of Madras; and finally, to the many individuals of the Sri Aurobindo *āśram* and library. Their interest and encouragement have frequently sustained this enterprise. Appreciation is expressed to Sri Ramesh C. Jain, my publisher, for the execution of the final work and, especially, to Ms. Janee Hunsucker, Washington, and Ms. Sally Sutherland, Berkeley, California, for their editorial assistance. I express acknowledgement to the editors of *International Philosophical Quarterly* and *Humanitas* for granting permission to use materials previously published in Chapter Two. Citations are listed in the Bibliography. I also thank my colleagues in the Department of Religion and Religious Education, the Catholic University of America, Washington, in affording me the time to research and write without the usual academic duties. Finally, I thank my friends at Washington's birthplace, Virginia, for offering me a congenial atmosphere within which to write and to approach more deeply the Indian experience of which I speak.

PART ONE

RABINDRANATH TAGORE

1861-1941

CHAPTER ONE

The Man: The Relational Personality

Rabindranath Tagore was born in 1861 within three revolutionary currents which were to carry Bengal, his home, and all India into the modern age.[1] These parallel but related movements—the religious, the socio-political and the literary—were a formative influence in his youth, though later as an adult he himself was to contribute substantially to them. Emerging from early 19th century Hinduism and especially within Bengal, these three upheavals were the first signs of a Hindu renaissance which found full expression in the 20th century. Because of the religious, socio-political and literary transformation

1. Autobiographical sources are: *My Reminiscences* (London : Macmillan & Co., Ltd., 1917) ; *My Boyhood Days*, trans. Marjorie Sykes (Calcutta : Visva-Bharti, 1940) ; *Lectures and Addresses*, comp. Anthony X. Soares (London : Macmillan & Co., Ltd., 1928). Several helpful biographies are: Marjorie Sykes, *Rabindranath Tagore* (London : Longmans, Green & Co., Ltd., 1943) ; V. Lesny, *Rabindranath Tagore, His Personality and Work*, trans. Guy McKeever Phillips (London : George Allen Unwin, Ltd., 1939) ; Krishna Kripalani, *Tagore: A Life* (New Delhi : Malancha, 1961) ; Edward Tompson, *Rabindranath Tagore: Poet and Dramatist* (London: Oxford University Press, 2nd edit., 1948) ; Buddhadeva Bose, *Tagore: Portrait of a Poet* (Bombay: University of Bombay, 1962).

taking place in India and in Bengal in particular, Tagore grew into a high relational personality. He developed in the course of the Hindu renaissance the widest possible outlook with universal human interests. These three movements dealt especially with change and continuity within the Indian tradition, and Tagore in the course of his life profoundly confronted change and continuity in his own experience and artistic expression. This confrontation was the basis and the call for a relational personality, a personality whose work Sri Aurobindo would describe as the "overpassing of borders."[2]

The religious environment of his youth was sharply defined by renaissance India as experienced in his family, in the Brahmo Samaj and in his approach to classical Hinduism. The Tagore family, one of the most cultured and creative in all Bengal at the time, was a household where art, literature, music, drama and philosophy from East and West found continual play. Although the independence and heterodoxy expressed by the family removed them from the mainstream of the general society, there was in it a freedom of life, freedom from creed and custom, which nurtured the young Rabindranath. His father, the saintly and learned Maharshi Devendranath, aloof and aristocratic, was a modernist, selective in his understanding of Hindu beliefs and customs. The Maharshi's father, Dwarkanath, was an associate of Ram Mohun Roy in the formation of the Brahmo Samaj, and the Maharshi himself was for a time drawn to it though later he formed another society for a new understanding of religious and philosophical Hinduism. The Maharshi gave a subtle direction to the development of the young Rabindranath; the son was to assimilate a contemplative spirit and a thirst for freedom from his father. One impressionable event for Rabindranath was a trip taken with his father to the Himalayas, a journey that became the paradigm of an eighty year search for new horizons.

Rabindranath was the youngest of fourteen children, many of whom soon became intellectual leaders in Bengal. Dwijendranath, twenty-one years older than his youngest

2. Quoted in V. S. Naravane, *Rabindranath Tagore: A Philosophical Study* (Allahabad: Central Book Depot, 1946), P. 3.

brother, was a philosopher and writer of philosophical poetry; Satyendranath was both a scholar, a translator of Sanskrit literature, and a judge who became the first Indian member of the Indian Civil Service; Jyotirindranath, the brother who actually brought up the youngest of the Tagores, was a playwright, a musician, an aesthete who made a living through business; a sister, Swarnakumani, wrote novels; and the wife of Satyendranath edited a popular Calcutta magazine. The young Rabindranath did not stand out in this creative atmosphere, and his shy and somewhat reflective nature became only gradually expressive. He was a restless youth, a dreamer who sang, participated in plays and composed some music. At the age of fourteen he began to write youthful sentimental poetry.

The Tagore family received its spirit from Ram Mohun Roy and the Brahmo Samaj movement. Roy was the first in the early 19th century to attempt a critique of Hinduism. Although open to the West and looked upon by some as an oriental-occidentalist, he sought to contain the traditional and cultic customs of Hinduism while broadening its humanitarian and social dimensions. He envisioned a broad synthesis of East and West. Rabindranath was inspired by Roy, for he too saw himself within a new cultural and spiritual age, an age not contained by convention and custom. Tagore assimilated Roy's spirit in his own effort toward harmony, harmony in the diverse facets of Indian experience. In 1885 he associated himself with the Brahmo Samaj but later separated from it. He knew Keshab Chandra Sen, the leader of the Brahmo Samaj after Roy, and from him gained the initiative to widen his religious and cultural interests.

As a youth Rabindranath was not intellectually rigorous. He had little formal schooling and had withdrawn from school by the age of fourteen; he was basically self-taught for his tutors were not too successful with him either. He went to England and studied law for two years but returned to India without a degree. As a young man his father put him in charge of the family country estates along the Padma river, where he lived on a houseboat, supervising and keeping records of his father's lands, writing poetry and confronting for the first time village India. The Padma river experience brought him into direct contact with the folk traditions, especially Bengali Vaiṣṇāvism. He quickly identified himself with the folk music, the Bhatiali river singers, the itinerant Baul singers, storytellers and village *kīrtans*, and began to assimilate the imagery and the lyricism, the personalism and eroticism of indigenous folk songs, and he never lost this identification with folk people and rural India. He continued to steep himself in Vaiṣṇāva poetry, meeting Vaiṣṇāva scholars and reading the poetry of Jayadeva, Vidyāpati and Caṇḍidās. The deep humanistic quality of Vaiṣṇāva religious expression was incorporated in his own developing poetry. But the unique lesson he learned from Vaiṣṇāvism was the transformation of human love into divine love, a quality found in all his future writings.

The Tagore family frequently sang the Vedic hymns and recited the *Upaniṣads*. From an early age Tagore was impressed by the breadth and depth of Upaniṣadic thought and its capacity to hold at the same time multiple world views and diverse experiences. He absorbed the universalism and the tolerance so pervasive in these sacred Hindu scriptures, and in his own literature he was able to embrace multiple perceptions, an absence of dogmatism, and an all-pervasive divine presence in nature. The *Upaniṣads* were the strongest classical Hindu influence upon him. Yet he approached the scriptures as a renaissance Indian: he was selective. He rejected the negativism of the *Upaniṣads* and was drawn to their positive aspects. By identifying joy as the most positive element of Upaniṣadic experience, he was later to develop an aesthetic unparalleled in contemporary Indian writing. In this early stage of his life, the religious formation of Tagore was defined significantly by the impetus of a new India as he gradually extended his relationships to men and movements, to literature and the aesthetic, to the past and the present.

The socio-political revolution taking place in India since the early 19th century, forging both a national and an international consciousness, affected everyone who entered the public arena. Tagore became involved with the freedom movement, called *swadeshi* in Bengal. His utmost political activity, however, was a short term as president of the provincial congress which he looked upon as a failure because his moves for rural improvement were rejected. Although close in friendship to Gandhi for half a century, Tagore openly opposed the Gandhian tactics of strikes, boycotts, marches and fasts to achieve political independence. In 1921 he spoke of *swarāj* (home-rule) as *māyā* (ephemeral reality) during Gandhi's all-India strike and stated that "*Swarāj* is not our objective. Our fight is a spiritual fight—it is for man."[3] He viewed non-violence in practice as a coercive and artificial means for reform rather than the creative means of human transformation which Gandhi intended it to be.

Tagore was to extend his social energies through a half century of work as an educator. He went to Bolpur, a village north of Calcutta, in 1901, to property that his father used as a retreat and meditation centre. There he was drawn to practical activities and to enter more deeply into the fullness of life than poetry had permitted him to do. In his own words it was a return "from my exile in a dream world,"[4] for it was within the school he established there that he discovered new relationships with children and colleagues and nature. Tagore had married and raised a family but his wife, a daughter and a son died at relatively early ages. These tragic events compelled him to seek relationships and service through education. He saw the building of the school as a divine incentive working in his life compelling him to practical service.[5] In the course of twenty years he had founded Santiniketan, an *āśram* school, Sriniketan, a school designed for rural and village uplift, and the international university, Visva-Bharati. At Sriniketan he was most directly concerned with social needs through programmes to establish cooperative societies, village crafts and cottage industries, and the practical dissolution of caste barriers. In no area of life did Tagore extend his energies and relational life more than in education.

The international consciousness which Tagore helped to create in India is one of his finest contributions to contemporary Indian society. He had personal contacts with a score of

3. Rabindranath Tagore, *Letters to a Friend,* ed. C. F. Andrews (New York: Macmillan Co., 1929), p. 128.
4. Rabindranath Tagore. *The Religion of Man* (Boston: Beacon Press, 1961), p. 166.
5. *Ibid.*

significant Westerners. Most closely associated with him at Santiniketan were Leonard Elmhirst, a British educationist, and C. F. Andrews, a British missionary who came to live and work intimately with Tagore. Numerous Europeans gave direction to his interests. The notion of an international university came to him in Japan during his conversation with Paul Richard; Romain Rolland, a European savant, instilled in Tagore the perception that Asia needed a pride in herself and suggested a centre for Eastern culture; Sylvain Levi urged the poet to focus on India's cultural influence on the Far East, a focus Tagore was most concerned with in his travels to China and Japan. In the course of time he had personal contacts with Bertrand Russell, Gilbery Murray, Einstein, Keyserling, Schweitzer and Bergson. His reading of Western writers was equally wide for the influence of Spencer, Darwin and Lamarck can be found in his evolutionary thought; T.H. Huxley, Creen Caird, William James and John Stuart Mill were also read by Tagore. Yet Tagore found more obvious enjoyment in and was more influened by Shelley, Wordsworth, Browning, Whitman and Thoreau. He came to develop ever widening loyalties to a people, a nation, the world and ultimately to universal man. In spite of this international awareness Ananda Coomaraswamy has concluded that Tagore was "essentially Indian in conception and appeal."[6]

As his career and international reputation advanced, Tagore began to travel throughout the world, an effort that increased as he grew older. He made several visits to China and Japan, attempting to harken these peoples to the common spirituality which all Asia shared. Travel brought him in personal contact with Buddhism which he always admired, and again he was to discover and speak of the most positive aspects in Buddhism, that is, the sympathy for living things, the friendship, the universal love and compassion taught by Lord Buddha. He travelled to England and North America where he lectured extensively. During these years he worte his finest essays on man, world and God. These travels, especially to the West, made him a champion of science, of democracy and economic development. In the final years of his life because of his Western

6. Naravane, p. 3.

experiences, he was to speak vigorously against imperialism and fascism. Thus Tagore developed an international reputation as poet and philosopher, preceptor and prophet. He became a symbol and an institution.[7]

By extending relational life Tagore embraced both the nation and the world—India, the Far East and the Western world; his concerns included national independence and spiritual self-rule, *āśram* education and village reform, and ultimately the brotherhood of all nations. His stance as poet resounded in his socio-political activities: namely, "bind yourself to no particular world."[8] At Santiniketan and among the Indian people in general he attempted to build a community which would recognize no geographical boundaries. "They will know only one country and that country will comprise the whole world. They will know only one race and that race will cover the entire human race."[9] Yet Tagore remained thoroughly an Indian and although the English conferred knighthood upon him, he rejected it in 1919 as a protest against the mindless massacre of innocent Indians at Jallianwalah Bagh in Amritsar. Contributing more to building of a global consciousness in India than any other Indian, he accomplished this task without a loss to his heritage and provincial concerns.

Although the religious and socio-political movements in the 19th and 20th centuries were deeply rooted in Bengal, it was in the literary revival in which the Bengalis assumed the greatest leadership. Bankim Chandra Chatterji, the creator of the Indian prose novel, was responsible for liberating the Bengali language and initiating a new literature. Bankim, drawing wholly from Hinduism, was soon followed by Michael Madhusudan Datta who introduced blank verse as an alternative to the couplet in Bengali poetry. Madhusudan, a Christian, reflected a clear Western emphasis. A lyric poet, Behari Lal Chakravarty tried to bring about a synthesis of Hindu and Westren poetry, and it was he who had the greatest

7. Bose, p. 12.

8. *Letters to a Friend*, p. 44.

9. Quoted in Santosh Chandra Sen Gupta, ed., *Rabindranath Tagore, Homage from Visva-Bharati* (Santiniketan: Visva-Bharati, 1962), p. 8.

influence on the young Tagore. These Bengali writers had rejected past literary models and given precision to the difference between tradition and convention in literature. Within this context Tagore emerged as the one figure who would eventually raise Bengali to a literary language recognized throughout India and the world.

The range and volume of his writing are vast. He wrote poetry most consistently, probably every day of his life. Over two thousand poems have been published and tor between two to three thousand songs he wrote both words and music. He wrote dramas, in prose and verse, novels, short stories, essays and journals. Although few of his letters have been published, he produced more letters than any other genre of literature. At the age of sixty he began to paint and by sixty-seven it had became a major occupation resulting in over three thousand paintings. He touched everything that the artistic hand could utilize as a medium of self-expression.

The extent of literary creativity indicates that Tagore looked upon writing as a *sādhana* (spiritual discipline) which was typical in the Hindu tradition. The Sanskrit word for literature is *sahitya*, that which unites. The primary function of literature was educative, it was a discipline which sought the inter-relationship between man, nature, cosmos and self realization. Tagore's literary work was not didactic but an educative process, a *sādhana* culminating in self-realization.

His poetry has been classified as devotional and dialogical or discursive and intuitive; it included love poems, nature poems, social, religio-mystical and even legendary-historical poems. He was a poet of many styles and periods and varieties of form, since his technical skill drew upon the full resources of the Bengali language. His contribution to Bengali literature was a lyric impulse for he was essentially a lyric poet who introduced new rhythms in Bengali poetry.[10] Tagore's basic models were the European Romantics and the Vaiṣṇāva poets as he tried to blend into his own work the folk song with a synthesis of classical Indian-Western poetry. In 1883 he published a volume titled *Prabhat Sangit* which immediately made him a major poet.

10. I am most indebted to Buddhadeva Bose for the literary insights here and to follow.

One poem in this volume, "The Awakening of the Waterfall", contained a theme that he would consistently pursue: namely, the extension of the individual into the universal life of humanity and nature. This was the germ of his future perceptions concerning relationship. His richest period extended from 1890 to 1910, a period in which he published eight volumes of poetry focusing upon the nature and interpenetration of man, nature, world and divinity. A mature moment in poetic creativity came with three hundred and seventy-six pieces, all of high consistency, written between 1906 and 1914, and published in three volumes *Gitanjali* (1910), *Gitimalya* (1914) *Gitali* (1914). His previous themes converge in this series, including love of nature, love of women and mankind, the dedication to nation and poetry and suffering, death and God. Instant recognition came to Tagore with the Nobel Prize in 1913, which was awarded for selections from the above volumes in an English translation titled *Gitanjali*. Some have considered *Balaka* as his finest poetic work, and it was within this series of poems that he dealt with the problem of change. He concluded that change is the essential constituency of reality.

At the age of twenty-two Tagore published his first volmue of essays on such subjects as friendship, evolution, the universe, human rights and death. His more philosophical prose on the meaning of nature, the self and aesthetics was soon to follow. His two most important philosophical essays are *Dharma* and *Santiniketan*, both written in Bengali and containing a high level of philosophical exploration. *Dharma* shows a strong Upaniṣadic influence while *Santiniketan* reflects Vaiṣṇāva influence. Tagore lectured extensively in the West between 1912-1913, and this resulted in a series of essays in English. *Sādhana*, culled from his previous *Santiniketan*, is a basic guide to his philosophy; *Personality* gives emphasis to the subjective element in understanding and the search for meaning; *Creative Unity* focuses upon the process of becoming in man, nature and the divine; *Religion of Man* covers the whole range of his thought; and *Man* is the most precise statement of Tagore's prevalent humanism.

The dramas, consisting of great variety from comedy to lyrical dance-dramas, and short stories and novels accumulated over the years. *Prakritir Pratishodh* was his first important play; in it he rejected asceticism as a life ideal and concluded that man must enter into the joy of nature and humanity for growth and realization. *Raja*, in English translated as "The King of the Dark Chamber," was one of Tagore's more philosophical dramas which expressed the interplay between the individual self and the absolute self. The poet enjoyed acting and would frequently appear in the plays himself.

In his literary work Tagore is very much the classical writer who introduces a folk and indigenous quality, and this is especially true in his short stories, novels and the epical *Gora*, his major fictional prose. But in his painting he becomes wholly impressionistic and modern. The paintings reveal a different man, a level of personality rarely found in his literature. They do not reflect the joy and the revelry and the brilliance of his poetry; they are pensive, moody and dark, and lack precision. They indicate a subconscious level of expression. He once reflected on the difference between his method of writing and method of painting as that which exists between rational and technical work, on the one hand, and following the mere movement of the hand and brush on the other.

India has produced prolific writers before, but no other Indian writer in the modern period has contributed so much to advance literature and language as Tagore. The fertile imagination and restless talent of Tagore continually sought new paths of expression. This quality, reflective of his total personality, is consonant with his basic life philosophy. The personality of the poet became increasingly relational as his life advanced and intensified in religious experience. He spoke several times of the initial experience, at the age of twenty-one while living on Sudder Street in Calcutta, which introduced him to a cosmic experience of all-embracing love. His closeness to the villages and the folk people, to children and to nature, were contexts for heightening his experiences throughout his life. The daily pattern of his life indicates not only a contemplative spirit but also an impatient anticipation for greater experience. He would awake at three or four each morning and silently await the breaking of the day, but once the day had begun his mind and spirit would move swiftly to a multiplicity of interests and projects.

A gradual transformation of personality was observable in his changing physical appearance. As a youth he was delicate and fastidious: his thirties revealed a stylish and aristocratic figure, with long black hair in ringlets, dressed elegantly; in his middle years he was the lean, short-bearded, somewhat priestly and pedantic figure; but as he grew old, with a face marked by age and work, success and sorrow, dressed in ground-length, brown, flowing robes, with a long white beard and hair, he struck an awesome presence. Buddhadeva Bose spoke of what impressed him most in Tagore : "It was the quality of *repose.* He was marvelously restful, always, marvelously controlled, always, without the slightest sign of the strain that fame and the processes of creation must have imposed upon him."[11]

The pattern of Tagore's life was the increasing network of interests, talents and accomplishments. His personality developed as his relational life expanded. He became the artist in the broadest sense of the word: the creator. To create, for him, was to experience and express relational life to the fullest. Tagore achieved this through confronting as much life as he could in his eighty years. He died in 1941 still painting and writing poems on man and death and immortality.

11. *Ibid.*, p. 17 ; see pp. 13-17 for Bose's description of Tagore.

CHAPTER TWO

His Thought: Ānanda Yoga

A vision of underlying harmony has been the consistent result of religious experience in the development of the Indian tradition. Rabindranath Tagore expressed this vision in his literature. He has been called "the supreme reconciler, harmonizer and peacemaker in the domain of modern thought" because the principle of harmony was so clearly pivotal to his philosophical outlook.[1] In Indian art *rasa* is the aesthetic sense which achieves a full expression of reality. For Tagore, however, all human experience contributed to a creative and more integral vision of reality; the principle of harmony and *rasa*, the aesthetic sense, pervaded all his life experiences. The development of an *ānanda-yoga* was the principal means through which the aesthetic sense was cultivated and universal harmony achieved. Tagore is now known to the world of letters as a follower of *ānanda-yoga*, the aesthetic path in achieving growth in consciousness. The path (*yoga*) was joy-filled (*ānanda*) because it elicited from him consistent creativity. In examining the levels of reality experienced by evolving man, by artistic man and by religious man respectively,

1. V. S. Naravane, *Modern Indian Thought* (Bombay: Asia Publishing House, 1964), p. 128. This work and Naravane's *Rabindranath Tagore: A Philosophical Study*, are the best philosophical studies on Tagore.

Tagore's philosophical humanism can be exposed and *ānanda-yoga* specified.

The basis for Tagore's philosophy of man rests upon the fact that man evolves from lower forms of life to become ultimately its highest expression. The experience of physical man consists in his relationship to things; since he is orientated externally, his primary interests lie in quantity, abundance and material goods. This level of human personality is especially practical for it is governed by principles of expediency and utility which seek self-aggrandizement. Physical man, according to Tagore, experiences reality as a specialist because his vision has been narrowed by the world of quantity. If he is to raise himself to the level of personal man, the individual must extend his relationships beyond quantity. Personal man advances from quantity to quality, from facts to truth, from necessity to choice, from utility to self-expression. When personal man extends his relationships in a qualitative manner, he contributes to his own evolution which consists in the growth of his inner life. Personal man, unlike the specialist on the physical level, might be called a universalist who is not confined to a narrow experience of reality. Since his aspirations are without limit, he strives to transcend limitations as he extends his personal relationships.

Tagore's perception of the relatedness within nature itself is revealed frequently in the construction of a nature scene, as in "The Wayfaring Path:"

> This is the wayfaring path. It leads from the forest to the road, through the road to the river-side, into the shade of the Banyan tree nestling by the side of the ferry. And then it goes winding from the broken edge of the opposite shore entering into a village; further, it passes the bordering linseed fields, by the shady mango-grove, along the edge of the lotus lake, close by the vehicle stand, to merge into what neighbouring village I do not know.[2]

The experience of the rhythm between man and nature is the

2. Tagore, *Lipika* (Bombay: Jaico Publishing House, 1969), p. 1.

basis for Tagore's vision of underlying harmony. In *Gitanjali* it is identified as an experience of life:

> The same stream of life that runs through my veins night and day runs through the world and dances in rhythmic measures. It is the same life that shoots in joy through the dust of the earth in numberless blades of grass and breaks into tumultuous waves of leaves and flowers.[3]

Experiencing harmony between man and the universe, Tagore spoke of "the bonds of friendship/With the universe" and that "For long has this earth given me/Her hospitality." Personal man extends relationships because he perceives the expanse of life beyond himself: "With the touch of life all matters mingle on their own accord with other matters in one unity of inseparable beauty."[4]

Experience is within the world of *māyā* (appearance). Avoiding the sharp dichotomy sometimes posited in Indian thought, Tagore viewed the world as the place of both truth and appearance. Since truth is found in relationships within the world of appearance, *māyā* holds truth within itself. Physical man, who relates to reality only in a quantitative manner, is limited to the world of appearance; on the other hand personal man experiences truth within the world of appearance because he relates to the world in a qualitative manner. For Tagore the world of appearance was personally relational wherein man had the capacity not only to transcend the quantitative dimensions of himself and his world but also to develop an infinity of relationships because of his aspirations. Striving to transcend limitations as he extends personal relationships, man becomes a universalist as his aspirations seek fulfilment; change, development and an evolving consciousness take place as he increases his personal relationships within this world.

One of Tagore's most original concepts emerges at this

3. Tagore, *Gitanjali*, trans. by author (London: Macmillan & Co., Ltd., Indian Edition, 1966), pp. 64-65.

4. Tagore, *Wings of Death*, trans, by Aurobindo Bose (London: John Murray, 1960), "Borderland," No. 13 & 14, pp. 36-37; also *Lipika*, "The Life and Mind," p. 113.

point: the surplus in man. Man has an enormous surplus far in excess of his physical requirements where his thoughts and aspirations have play. The area of surplus is the limitless potentiality of the human personality. Herein lies the infinite future of man. Man enters the evolutionary process as an incomplete being but as he extends his relational life he begins to transcend his incompleteness. On the physical level he extends his relationships to reality in a strictly quantitative manner; on the personal level he lives and relates to reality within the world of appearance; drawing upon his surplus he experiences the inner-relatedness of reality. The rhythm and underlying harmony of life are experienced at this profound level of relational existence. As he draws upon the surplus within himself, he experiences reality as an artist and as religious man. Moreover, he expresses his experience best in terms of art and religion. The surplus, manifesting itself in the religious consciousness of man, is joy-filled (*ānanda*) and meaningful:

> Religion can have no meaning in the enclosure of mere physical and material interest; it is in the surplus we carry around our personality—the surplus which is like the atmosphere of the earth, bringing to her a constant circulation of lıght and life and delightfulness.[5]

The surplus in man is the source of human creativity. Artistic expressions and productions originate in the surplus which impels him toward creative life. Tagore, however, was unable to define art with precision. Even so his descriptions reveal a deep understanding of the nature of man. Art is the "response of man's creative soul to the call of the Real."[6] It is that which is most perfectly shareable. It expresses a "unity by which this world is realized as humanly significant to us."[7] The source of art is disclosed: "Wherever man meets man in a living relationship, the meeting finds its natural expression in the works of art, the signatures of beauty, in which the mingling

5. Tagore. *The Religion of Man* (Beacon Press: Boston, 1961), p. 45.
6. *Ibid.*, p. 13o.
7. *Ibid.*, p. 132.

of the personal touch leaves its memorial."[8] Tagore identified the nexus between art and human creativity, namely, living relationships. The artist "must establish harmonious relationship with all things with which he has dealings."[9] Creativity consists in the modulation of these relationships. Tagore's most astute understanding of art is found in an essay on the nature of the artist:

> We can make truth ours by actively modulating its inner-relations. This is the work of art; for reality is not based in the substance of things but in the principle of relationship.[10]

Within relational experience the artist has materials for expression. To expess himself as an artist, man brings to this complex of inter-relationships a modulation of vision which consists in the creative process of imaging forth the expression. Within the creative process, *rasa*, the aesthetic taste and perception, is evoked. This is the moment of aesthetic intuition. Aesthetic knowledge and intuition in classical Indian thought take place in man's higher reason and the creative process is the work of this higher reason. In the imaging of relational life in poetry, music, painting and literature, the artist of Tagore's conception expresses himself creatively. Art results from the modulation of relationships, which, in fact, is the actual imaging forth of relational life. To seek harmony in multiplicity may well have been the goal of Indian aestheticians. *Rasa* has been the essential element in Indian art and aesthetic experience. But Tagore's insight into the relational nature of reality and experience specifies the work of the artist and the function of *rasa* more precisely, The harmonious and integral vision of artistic expression is the imaging forth of relational life which the aesthetic sense, the *rasa*, has caught for a brief moment.

Since the surplus in man rests in his personality, creativity is

8. Tagore, *Creative Unity* (London: Macmillan & Co., Ltd., Indian Edition, 1962), p. 115.
9. *The Religion of man*, p. 133.
10. *Ibid.*, p. 134. See pp. 133-134 for Tagore's use of the terms modification and modulation of relationships; both terms seem to have been used interchangeably in this context.

the conscious expression of the personality. The personal dimension of art, according to Tagore, is the expression of personality, the self-expression of the artist. Tagore's concept of personality has far reaching implications for both his aesthetic theory and his concept of man. He defined personality as:

> . . . a self-conscious principle of living unity; it at once comprehends and yet transcends all the details of facts that are individually mine, my knowledge, feelings, wish and will, my memory, my hope, my love, my activities, and all my belongings.[11]

This suggests that the whole man enters into the work of creative expression. Art is the creation of the human personality because personality brings to consciousness the individual's relationships to reality. Knowledge is to know things in their relatedness. To know reality in its relatedness is to know the truth of things, and to have a knowledge of things is to know them in their relation to the greater universe. Thus personality, for Tagore, is a category of human consciousness. The initial level of consciousness is somewhat negative for it consists in an awareness of distinction, individuality and all that separates man from his world and individual man from his neighbour; but the positive aspect of personality, a higher level of consciousness, is the medium for communication and self-expression. Personality discloses relationships and creativity expresses this reality in art when one functions on a higher level of consciousness. Because a "principle of uninterrupted relation" is the structure of personality on this level of consciousness, art becomes an expression of personality itself.[12] Within

11. Tagore, "The Religion of an Artist," *Contemporary Indian Philosophy*, ed. S. Radhakrishnan & J. H. Muirhead (New York: Macmillan Co., 1936), pp. 36-37. Note in this place: "Limitation of the unlimited is personality; God is personal where he creates."
12. Tagore, *Sādhana* (London: Macmillan & Co., Ltd., Indian Edition, 1965), p. 42. Tagore attributed the activity of the personality in its capacity to relate man to nature and the universe to the indigenous genius of India. See *Sādhana*, pp 8-9 : "In India men are enjoined to be fully awake to the fact that they are in the closest relation to things around them, body and soul, and that they are to hail the morning sun, the flowing water, the fruitful earth, as the manifestation of the same living truth which holds them in its embrace."

the context of personality, then, a definition of art can be reconstructed from Tagore's thought: art is the modulation of relationships brought to consciousness in the personality of man.

Personality has the capacity to transform all that is presented to it. In the artistic expression, however, something of the personality also gets communicated. Although man expresses something extrinsic to himself in the artistic subject, he expresses at the same time something of himself too. The highest function of life, according to Tagore, is the communication of personality. Art becomes a deeper response of man to reality as it becomes a greater medium for the expression of individual personality.

Man responds creatively to his experiences because he is by nature an artist. Tagore's unique contribution to both the philosophy of art and the philosophy of man may be his view that man is by nature an artist. He perceived an instinctive urge in man towards a continual "transformation of facts into human imagery."[13] Within experience man creatively perceives, integrates and transforms relational life. The almost rhythmical movement of perception, integration and transformation appears frequently as the structural framework for Tagore's stories and novellas. The classical musical form of exposition, development and variation, and recapitulation, found in the composition of Bengali music and accommodated in Tagore's literature, is similar to the aesthetic process of perception, integration, and transformation. Tagore saw this process unfolding in the natural development of social life. Exposition, development and variation in musical form correspond to perception and integration in the aesthetic process; again recapitulation in the first corresponds to transformation in the secord.

Tagore spoke of the sympathy with which the artist must approach the world and seek participation within it; he considered this sensitivity as part of the Indian heritage. If man

13. *The Religion of Man*, p. 133. In this place Tagore explicitly says, "For man by nature is an artist." Also see the essay "The Religion of an Artist," and the first chapter of *Personality* (London: Macmillan & Co., Ltd., 1965), "What is Art ?"

is to perceive the meaning of relational life, a sensitivity which draws him into participation in life is imperative. Yet for integration to take place the individual must bring his imagination to bear upon dispersive insights and perceptions. Imagination brings before the mind the vision of man's greater being and its work culminates in love and joy. V. S. Naravane considers Tagore's aesthetic experience as typical of Bengali Vaiṣṇāvism for it is the outcome of a primeval joy continually overflowing and manifesting itself.[14] Tagore looked upon joy as validating the realization of truth: "Gladness is the one criterion of truth, and we know when we have touched truth by the music it gives, by the joy of greeting it sends forth to the truth in us."[15] Thus within the processes of perception and integration man functions as an artist because all his sensitivities—sympathy, participation, joy and love—integrate him in his relationships. Again, the principle of harmony which is central to Tagore's thought finds expression in art and literature. The aesthetic sense, *rasa*, is also operative in the process of integration. According to Bharata, an early Indian aesthetician, *rasa* is the interaction between subjective dispositions and the object culminating in the intuition from which art and literature result.[16]

Within the aesthetic process of perception and integration, the transformation of relationships takes place. Although perceived at first as disparate, the experiences of relationship bring a change and a transformation to life. As a storyteller Tagore was concerned primarily with the transformation of human relationships: in fact, his fiction may well have this as its objective. A clear example exists in his novel, *Binodini*, in which the development of the story consists not only in the interaction between the leading characters but also in the actual transformation of their relationships. In Tagore's literary tragedies, failure in human life is the direct result of a character's inability to transform the relationships in which he finds himself.

14. Naravane, *Rabindranath Tagore : A Philosophical Study*, p. 152.

15. *The Religion of Man*, p. 107.

16. John Britto Chethimattam, "Rasa, The Soul of Indian Art," *International Philosophical Quarterly*, Vol. X, No. 1 (1970), p. 52.

Transformation as an element of human growth is part of the artistic process itself.

Tagore found it impossible to separate the creativity expressed in art from the whole of life. The pursuit of art for him is the pursuit of life. He envisioned art and life forming an integral whole. There is no sharp division between them because art emerges from the deepest experiences of man and reflects the highest expressions of life. Amiya Chakravarty views Tagore's short stories in particular as an effort to express "the weddedness of life or the sense of the whole."[17] The artist by integrating and transforming relationships overcomes multiplicity. It could be for this reason that Tagore saw art as part of everyone's life:

> It is the duty of every human being to master, at least to some extent, not only the language of intellect, but also that personality which is the language of Art. It is a great world of reality for man,—vast and profound,—this growing world of his own creative nature. This is the world of Art.[18]

Man is by nature an artist, and it is art which completes man by bringing him to an experience of the wholeness of life.

Tagore's experience of religion was indistinguishable from his experience as poet, dramatist and artist. In an essay titled "The Religion of an Artist" he gave expression to his notion of religion:

> My religion is essentially a poet's religion. Its touch comes to me through the same unseen and trackless channels as does the inspirations of my music. My religious life has followed the same mysterious line of growth as has my poetical life.[19]

17. See "Introduction" by Amiya Chakravarty, *The Housewarming and Oiher Selected Writings*, trans. Mary Lago, Tarun Gupta and Amiya Chakravarty (New York: New American Library, 1965), p. viii. In the same place Chakravarty writes "...Tagore was exposed to natural correlations; different techniques of artistic representation revealed not only parallels but an integral vision."
18. *Creative Unity*, p. 197.
19. "The Religion of an Artist," p. 32.

This implies that religious experience, for Tagore, results from the whole of life; art and religion form a harmonious and integral experience. Religion is neither relegated to one area of life nor reserved to one dimension of man, it is an experience which draws upon and is an expression of the whole man.

Nowhere in Tagore's thought do his humanism and Vaiṣṇāva background appear more clearly than in his views of religion. In Vaiṣṇāva poetry Tagore found religious experience that was ostensibly sensitive: "But my imagination was fully occupied with the beauty of their forms and the music of their words; and their breath, heavily laden with voluptuousness, passed over my mind without distracting it."[20] Reflecting upon the poet's religion, Buddhadeva Bose calls it a sensuous spirituality.[21] Religious man for Tagore draws upon all human sensitivity in order to experience the divine in humanity; he enters with feeling, emotion and passion into the finite world.

When man begins to seek the truth of his higher personality within relational life, he establishes himself as a religious man. A religious experience, for Tagore, reveals a sense of universal personality. The realization of man in his universality is the truth of his higher personality. The gradual self-realization of universal humanity is the path of liberation which concerns religious man. Tagore was aware of the transcendental truth within man, the Universal and Supreme Man, and spiritual life for him was the renunciation of the individual self for the sake of the supreme self. He did not negate individuality in the process for it was his experience that "My religion is in the reconciliation of the super-personal man, the universal human spirit, in my own being."[22]

Religious consciousness, according to the poet, is achieved

20. *Ibid.*, pp. 29-30.

21. Bose, p. 94. See *Letters to a Friend*, p. 131, where Tagore speaks of "the life-throb of God's reality," felt by the poet.

22. Chakravarty, ed., *A Tagore Reader* (Boston: Beacon Press. 1961), p. 113. Also see *Wings of Death*, "Recovery," No. 25, p. 79, which speaks to the universal spirit in individual man: "The unuttered words in the vast mind of Man/Wander through space like nebulae./Striking against the boundary of my mind./They condense, take form,/And revolve round my study."

in the love relationship between *paramātman* (universal self) and the *jīvātman* (individual self). The personality of religious man is fulfilled in the same manner as are other levels of life: namely, in relationships. A twofold relationship raises man in his conscious experience of reality: his relationship to the finite and his relationship to the infinite. Although the truth of the higher personality is the consciousness of the relationship with the infinite, it is rooted in the world and in history. Within the created order man achieves:

> . . . the vision of the infinite in all forms of creation, in the human relationship of love: to feel it in the air we breathe, in the light in which we open our eyes, in the water in which we bathe, in the earth on which we live and die.[23]

There is the possibility of encounter with the infinite whenever man meets man, whenever man enters significantly into nature. A description of religion in Tagore's thought can be drawn from this context: namely, the realization of universal personality that is achieved through the conscious experience of relationship to the infinite encountered in the midst of creation.

Since man is multi-dimensional, evolving, artistic and religious, he experiences the world as creative and the divine as Creator. The more conscious he becomes of the inter-relationships of the created order, the closer he approaches the divine principle of unity that constitutes the inter-relationship of things. Religious man not only encounters the divine in creation, but he also encounters it as Creator, as Divine-Artist. The Creator-Artist manifests his infinity, now modified, in the world of man. Tagore's humanism is highlighted by a God deeply involved in the human order. He could candidly sing: "I send my salutations to the God of Humanity."[24] Creation is the expression of the Creator-Artist, the Infinite Personality, who seeks continual self-expression. The divine, who is similar to man, stands incomplete and unfulfilled unless he finds expression. The personality of the divine is fulfilled as is the per-

23. *Personality*, p. 138.
24. Tagore, *A Flight of Swans, Poems from Balak*, (London : John Murray, 2nd edition, 1962), trans. Aurobindo Bose, No. 46, p. 114.

sonality of man: in the growth of relationships. As the Creator-Artist expresses himself in creation, his relationships are extended and the divine principle of unity is manifested in the created order.

Religious man is by nature an artist because he is made in the image of the Creator-Artist. He imitates and participates in the work of the Creator-Artist. Since religious man instinctively imitates the Creator-Artist, he *re-presents* the work of the Creator and thus participates in the creative process. Man imitates the divine in order to complete and fulfil himself. Man in his creative response to reality seeks to follow the example of the creator. He responds as an image-maker. Tagore drew upon the classical notion of *līlā* (play) by reflecting that the world as an art is the play of the supreme person revelling in image-making.[25] Man participates in the divine play for it is part of his nature and destiny. In a group of poems titled *Balaka*, written during the First World War, the theme of man's participation in the divine *līlā* (play) recurs continually. Life is *lilā*, "a play of joy and suffering," and a "play of forms."[26] Tagore looked upon religious man as taking to himself the Creator's work and becoming a participator in the creative process. Religious man seeks to build a universe in truth and beauty, a creation that is permanent and stable. In art he seeks to *re-present* the universal and transcendental experience, and in his imitation of the Creator-Artist he gives affirmation to the eternal even as he strives to *re-present* it.

Religious man is called to a second birth whereby he aspires to enter into the work of creation; he is called to the creative process. Man shares creativity with God as his personality is fulfilled. He attains this fulfilment only through a consciousness of "an extended vision of his true self."[27] This is achieved most radically through a consciousness of the relationship between the supreme soul and the soul of all created things. The "I" of man confronts the infinite "I," and in this relationship takes place the play of love between creature and Creator. In an essay titled "Second Birth," Tagore showed

25. "The Religion of an Artist," p. 38.

26. *A Flight of Swans*, No. 43, pp. 106-107.

27. *Sādhana*, p. 54.

that life is given meaning only in relationship: "... the soul's birth in the spiritual world is not the severance of relationship with what we call nature, but freedom of relationship, perfectness of relationship."[28] Man looks to union with the divine, but to be reborn into this union means full consciousness of relational life, finite and infinite. When consciousness is truly transformative, man is raised beyond his limitations and is no longer confined by finite existence.

Rasa in Indian thought also has transformation as its objective. The *Vedas* contain the notion of *rasa* and the earliest poets distinguished it from *harṣa*, the joy and exhaltation sought in the artistic work itself. The aesthetician Abhinavagupta, a tenth century Kashmir *Śaiva*, combined the earlier notion of *rasa* and *harṣa* which resulted in the classical aesthetic concept. In this synthesis *rasa* had been lifted from the level of the concrete and the particular to the level of the universal and the self-transcendent. It was no longer limited to just an aesthetic feeling and sense but had become analogous to an experience of release from the *samsaric* world. *Rasa* in later aesthetic theory appropriated the bliss of aesthetic experience to transcendental experience. In short the notion of *rasa* was no longer limited to mere aesthethic experience, but within the subjective order it was a vision of the *Ṛta*, the principle of cosmic harmony, that Indian aestheticians had experienced.[29] This was Tagore's experience and perception. His notion of spiritual rebirth consists in the fact that man is no longer bound to the facticity and particularity of concrete relationships; the personality of man is freed from the particular and achieves a self-transcendency and universality.

The fine arts for Tagore were spiritual disciplines. Reflecting the integral conception of man in the *Upaniṣads* and the Vaiṣṇāva poets who exemplified art as a spiritual discipline, Tagore envisioned the universal man brought into being through art. The aesthetic experience became for him a disci-

28. *Personality*, p. 94.
29. See Philp Rawson, *Indian Sculpture* (New York: E. P. Dutton & Co., 1966), pp. 120-131; Krishna Chaitanya, *A New History of Sanskrit Literature* (Bombay: Asia Publishing House, 1962), pp. 23 and 53 ; John Chethimattam, "Rasa, The Soul of Indian Art." pp. 44 and 62.

pline integrating man in his search for meaning. Among the *puruṣārthas* (goals of life), *kama* (desire) was looked upon not only as the fulfilment of passion and emotion but also as the development of aesthetic and artistic qualities. Once *kāma* was spiritualized by the *bhakti* (love) tradition in India, it became the goal that satisfied man's desire and his aspiration for the divine. The goal of *kāma*, raised now to the aesthetic and spiritual level, becomes the duty (*dharma*) of artistic man. Tagore had a strong continuity with the Indian tradition because he exemplified that aesthetic experience is a spiritual path for those who can integrate their lives with this discipline,

Tagore's total philosophy is an attempt to articulate *ānanda-yoga* as a path of salvation. His essays are the most serious discourse on the subject in contemporary Hinduism. He saw his own pursuit of *ānanda* as the effort of his life: "This has been the subject on which all my writings have dwelt—the joy of attaining the Infinite within the finite."[30]

30. Quoted in Naravane, *A Philosophical Study*, p. 53.

CHAPTER THREE

Educational Theory

In an amusing parable, '*The Parrot's Training*', Tagore executes a devastating parody on the condition of education. A golden cage is constructed for an exquisitely plumed parrot. All who are concerned with the parrot and the building of the extravagant cage flourish as satisfaction redounds to the owners and the beauty of their home is enhanced. The caged parrot, however, gradually dissipates. In this parable the cage is education, its builders are the educators and the parrot is the student. The story contains a preception of education that Tagore had had early in his life: namely, the need for freedom and cultural surroundings in human development.

The origin of his educational theory was his own home life and the freedom he had experienced within it. Withdrawing early from formal education and maintaining that "whatever I learned I have learned outside of class,"[1] the poet's own education was to come from the total environment of life. When the time came to educate his own children, he did not send them to conventional schools but educated them at home with the help of several tutors. Thus the genesis of Tagore's educational theory lay not in a new theory of learning but in recalling his own boyhood days. Since his memory of school

1. Tagore, "Rabindranath Tagore in Russia, *Visva-Bharati Bulletin*, No. 15, Nov. 1930, p. 28.

was that of an educational prison disassociated from the context of life, he sought a form of learning that would be linked organically to the whole of life, the people, the land and its culture.

Beginning his work in education at the turn of the century around the age of forty as he grew less satisfied with the sole occupation of writing, he sought public service and more active work. His creativity throughout the course of eighty years was directed toward personality development, literary, musical and artistic work, and toward education upon which he would place the greatest emphasis. He wrote an essay, *Siksar Herpher*, in 1892 in which he began a critique of the system of education then existing in India. Pointing out its defects, he judged that it made no adequate preparation for Indian culture and gave no inspiration to the Indian mind. In this same essay, moreover, he enunciated the pivotal principle that education must be a process of creative joy. Over the years he would speak out against anything alien, materialistic and impractical which the British system or any theory of education would advance. In these early years of reflection on Indian education, years preceded by the development of his socio-political thought, he advocated the principle of self-determination in the education of the masses. He was adamant that education must be in the hands of the people and their communities and not passed down by government. By the turn of the century Tagore had made a comprehensive critique of Indian education, the first statement and the clearest statement for the next fifty years.

Emerging as a prophet of an educational renaissance in India, he believed that "The widest road leading to the solution of all our problems is education."[2] He began to reflect on the best educational thought of the world, past and present. He was aware of the innovations brought out by Rousseau, Froebel, Pestalozzi and Herbart who all tried to release education into the area of life-experiences. Although he considered the history of naturalism in education as a unique moment in

2. Quoted in H.B. Mukherjee, *Education for Fulness: A Study of the Educational Thought and Experiment of Rabindranath Tagore* (Bombay: Asia Publishing House, 1962), p. 154.

its development, there is no evidence that he was directly influenced by Rousseau or even by John Dewey, the latter of whom he had met but whom he had preceded in terms of working out an educational theory. Among Indian educators he was the most outstanding figure in the first half of this century for he also preceded both Gandhi and Sri Aurobindo and did not ever imitate a foreign system or theorist. Tagore's theory is distinctive. Yet he sought a synthesis of East and West in both ideals and methods. His theory is marked by a synthetic, naturalistic, aesthetic and international character. These characteristics found their genesis in the perceptions he had of his personal development.

Tagore's writing on education would fill five volumes, with at least one hundred and thirty separate essays, pamphlets, addresses and a number of textbooks.[3] His basic philosophy of life emerges as does his educational philosophy from this body of writing. "The highest mission of education," he wrote "is to help us realize the inner principle of unity of all knowledge and all the activities of our social and spiritual being."[4] True education is the realizatoin of an inner quality of man, a realization that places human life in harmony with all existence. Education is not primarily didactic but leads to the attainment of a level of life in harmony with the universe. Tagore has described this ideal as the full growth of the individual in harmony with the universal, the Supreme Person who has in himself the various levels of consciousness and experience corresponding to man's physical self, life, mind and

3. Tagore wrote no single book on education but published essays on education in a number of journals, especially *The Visva-Bharati Quarterly* (Santiniketan), *Modern Review* (Calcutta), *Visva-Bharati News* and *Visva-Bharati Bulletin* (Santiniketan). Several good studies have been done on Tagore's educational thought, the most complete and definitive is H. B. Mukherjee, *Education for Fulness*; also contributive are Sunil Chandra Sarkar, *Tagore's Educational Philosophy and Experiment* (Santiniketan: Visva-Bharati, 1961); R. Tagore & Leonard K. Elmhirst, *Rabindranath Tagore: Pioneer in Education* (London: John Murray, 1961); A. V. Suryanarayana, *Tagore as Educationist* (Madras: M.S.R. Murty & Co., 1962); and Sasadhar Sinha, *Social Thinking of Rabindranath Tagore* (Bombay: Asia Publishing House, 1962).

4. *Creative Unity*. p. 199.

soul.[5] He recognized that India was endowed with the special power of binding together and had always highlighted the harmony of the individual and the universe. Drawing upon a synthetic conception of human development, Tagore saw education as the harmonization of the various elements of man's being. On the other hand if the harmony and unity of the whole man is lost, his inner *dharma* (law) is destroyed.

The realization of harmony is specified in Tagore's educational idealism as the pursuit of fullness (*bhūma*), the pursuit of the whole man. *Bhūman* is a Sanskrit noun meaning abundance, wealth and immensity, which he employed to best describe the ideal. Only man can pursue and ultimately realize *bhūma*, that immensity with the deepest self as distinguished from the surface self or the ego. Tagore viewed education as the process for evolving new patterns of life culminating in the realization of Universal Man. It is for this reason that education for Tagore took account of the organic wholeness of human individuality. There is a unity, a harmony, a wholeness sought in education whereby no separation of relationships exists in the perfection of the intellectual, spiritual and physical aspects of man. Tagore sought an education that was in touch with the whole of life: economic, intellectual, aesthetic, social and spiritual. Most fundamentally man must be in touch with his physical and natural environment. Although many of the villagers were technically illiterate, Tagore thought that folk education in India was always one with the life of the people. It made th evillagers conscious of social structures and relationships, village culture and even a wider culture, through the recitation of the epics, the *Purāṇas* and the participation in *Kīrtan-s*. Tagore employed the same principle in judging literature; that is, how universal is a particular piece of literature ? He sought a wholeness in his own writing, which sought the fullest expression of life.

The pursuit of *bhūma* is both individual and social. It seeks an inner and individual perfection, on the one hand, and the realization of an expanding social awareness and function on the other. In Tagore's literature there is a vast amount that

5. Sunil Chandra Sarkar, *Tagore's Educational Philosophy and Experiment*, p. 24.

reaches beyond the personal and the individual; his prose is most often a pursuit of fullness on the level of society. Human growth through education is, consequently, a movement toward greater wholeness. Tagore's most important aim in education is the development of the individual leading to a harmonious growth of personality. The development of the personality to fullness is also the core of his basic philosophy of life: "To attain full manhood is the ultimate end of education; everything else is subordinate to it."[6]

Fullness as an educational ideal is achieved by means of relationships. Tagore realized that unless his relationship with the wider world of humanity grew, his relationship with his *āśram* school would not be perfect. His singular insight in educational theory may well be that education is completed in the development of human relationships. Again, Tagore brought a general principle of life into education for ". . . the true meaning of living is outliving, it is ever growing out of itself."[7] When man realizes his individuality he is stimulated to growth by establishing wider relationships with a larger number of individuals and within an expanding context. Through individuality man achieves universality; relationship is thus realized in one's own being. Education becomes a bi-polar process, a dialectic, as one personality encounters another. Tagore would encourage his students to read world literature in order to understand how men had established relationships with the world and had achieved an intimacy with the cosmos. He had a sense of the correlation of phenomena which had its legitimacy and norm rooted in Hindu culture. To establish relationships was India's great endeavour, the Hindu tradition consistently sought the most distant connections in the world of phenomena as it attempted to extend human aspiration and achievement universally. For Tagore self-extension constitutes fuller humanity and in education, especially, man consciously extends himself by thought, sight, sound and imagination in relations of affection. In relationships does man become more fully educated.

6. Mukherjee, p. 267.

7. Tagore, *Thoughts from Rabindranath Tagore* (London: Macmillan & Co., Ltd., 1933), p. 37.

Freedom, sympathy and joy are also constitutive of Tagore's educational thought and the more immediate goals in extending relational life toward a pursuit of fullness. He observed that "The founding of my school had its origin in the memory of that longing for the freedom of consciousness, which seems to go back beyond the skyline of my birth."[8] Childhood, for Tagore, was a time of feeedom, freedom from specialization, freedom from social and professional conventionalism. In an essay titled "My School," he said that the object of education is the freedom of the mind which is achieved through a path of freedom. To speak of freedom as a path is to conceive of it as a formative discipline drawing mind, heart and will, into a liberation from ignorance, passion and prejudice, and the laws of entropy. Man, for Tagore, creates his own world and in the process is liberated. Education most simply is that which liberates. "Only through freedom can man attain his fullness of growth," wrote the poet,[9] and perfect freedom lies in the harmony of relationships which man realizes in his own being. Freedom (*mokṣa*) is the ideal at the heart of India's spiritual history for man's highest aspiration has been the realization of the relationship between his deepest self (*ātman*) and the Absolute (*Brahman*). In Tagore's conception of education, the freedom principle liberates the powers and energies of the personality to relate the individual with the universe, nature, man and finally Universal Man.

Two distinctive elements that Tagore brings to education are sympathy and joy. The development of feelings and emotions and the expansion of sympathy received a high place among his educational values. If man is to attain full personality, sympathy with all forms of life and experience is necessary. Tagore sought a close and intimate contact between the student and nature, believing that such contact brought about an expansion of sympathy. In fact, much that he urged in terms of natural environment was education in sympathy. Education in India during his youth was a "joyless education,"[10] and he

8. *The Religion of Man*, p. 172.
9. Tagore, "The Schoolmaster," *The Modern Review*, Vol. XXVI, No. 4, October, 1924, p. 372.
10. Tagore, *Towards Universal Man* (London: Asia Publishing House, 1961), p. 40.

sought a corrective. *Ānanda-yoga* is most descriptive of the poet's personality, and it is also his most original contribution to educational theory. He considered "work wedded to joy" as the best work.[11] The problem in education is to wed joy to knowledge. According to Tagore all life relationships are to fulfil knowledge or need or joy. Relational reality has joy as an inherent quality, for he wrote:

> I have a relationship with the world which is deeply personal. . . All our relationships with facts have an infinite medium which is Law, *Satyam*; all our relationship with truth has an infinite medium which is Reason, *Jnanam*; all our personal relationship has an infinite medium which is Love, *Anandam*.[12]

Truth, knowledge and joy are constitutive of reality as they are constitutive of the divine person. Growth in sympathetic joy is, consequently, a dominant principle in Tagore's educational thought. He discovered in his own experience and lived out over a lifetime the educational principles he enunciated. Experience confirmed him in the principles which later were collaborated to a great extent by Indian and Western educators.

The school only lays a seed for human development and is not its foundation. Dispensing with everything that was inessential, Tagore tried to create a particular atmosphere in his school. An atmosphere filled with living aspiration was far more important to him than classroom teaching or reading the great books. "For atmosphere there must be," he wrote, "for developing the sensitiveness of soul, for affording mind its true freedom of sympathy."[13] More important than academic growth was the building of culture, of atmosphere and vocation. This was accomplished by providing an environment that was natural, open and free, simple and primitive, and within a communal context.

11. Mukherjee, p. 366.
12. *Thoughts from Rabindranath Tagore*, p. 19.
13. Tagore, "Thoughts on Education," *The Visva-Bharati Quarterly*, Education Number, ed. Kshitis Roy, Vol. XII, Parts I & II, May-Oct. 1947, p. 2.

The union of man and nature is a major theme in Sanskrit poetry, and the same theme is pursued by Tagore in his poetry. He discovered a link between the different aspects of nature whose controlling principle was deeply felt by him. Nature was extremly wide: the animate world of trees, flowers and birds, the world of the physical universe with its forces and energies. It has been said that Tagore raised nature to the status of companion with whom one can enter into intimacy through aesthetic imagination and appreciation. Nature provided a profound and ecstatic delight to him. Believing that the pulse of nature quickens the spirit of the child, he viewed education outside it as harmful. A child should be surrounded by nature and natural objects for they have their own educational value. The child should be given the freedom to celebrate nature, "learning to see fire, air, water, land and the whole universe as pervaded by a universal consciousness. . ."[14] Tagore believed that for the first seven years a child's education should be left to nature because what a child needs most is freedom in nature in order to love it. Since a child abstracted from natural surroundings could not mature adequately, education divorced from the soil had little meaning for him. As such the true basis for Tagore's learning environment was an atmosphere of creative activity in the midst of nature where enquiry and feeling found full scope, formal teaching being the least significant aspect of education.

The poet designed his first school as an *āśram* community, modelled along the lines of the forest colonies of ancient India. It was in the classical forest communities (*tapovanas*) that Indian civilization began, and man's goal was "in realizing, in enlarging his consciousness by growing with and growing into his surroundings."[15] The *tapovana*, located in nature and communal in organisation, is the spiritual community of which the poet Kālidāsa sings. The Indian mind had developed through a close contact with nature and the aspiration of man to be one with the natural universe around him. Tagore's per-

14. Tagore, "The Problem of Education," quoted in Mukherjee, *Education for Fulness*, p. 36.

15. Tagore, "The Relation of the Universe and the Individual," *The Modern Review*, Vol. XIV, No. 1, July 1913, p. 1.

ception is that at every step in understanding and knowledge man must have an organic link with his surroundings. The *tapovana* man sought "a realization completely comprehensive."[16] Tagore considered the atmosphere of the *āśram* necessary if the religious spirit in the modern world was to find its power and expression. He believed that the *āśrams* of ancient India gave an answer to instilling the religious spirit. Santiniketan was established on the outskirts of a small town with surrounding villages wherein the sympathy for nature was quite visible.

The school of Tagore's conception may be described as open, free, abundant and spontaneous where young people could be free in spite of themselves. Education should not be heavy or burdensome or abstract There were no desks, chairs or classrooms in his first school. Laying no stress on knowledge through books, he emphasized learning directly from nature, life and the teacher. He believed that children should be free "to organize their own immediate environment." "Let the child never tire in his efforts to give play to his creative joy by inventing things with the help of whatever material lies ready at hand,"[17] he wrote. In his short stories the child figure matures by being left to nature and by being encouraged to find his own ways of facing the world. Mini in "The Cabuliwallah" and Phatik in "The Homecoming" are examples of children growing into a free and open world. "The Child's Return" and "The Crescent Moon" similarly reflect this capacity of the child. Tagore was convinced that in the early years, in particular, the child should come to truth through a natural process, spontaneously, through persons and things. The widest possible outlook and universal human interests would emerge in this way. Learning for the child was explorative, active and joyous: "For our perfection we have to be vitally savage and mentally civilized; we should have the gift to be natural with nature and human with human society."[18] The

16. Tagore, "A Poet's School," *Visva-Bharati Quarterly*, Vol. IV, No. 3, Oct. 1926, p. 199.

17. Tagore, *Ashrama Education* (Santiniketan: Visva-Bharati, n.d.), p 4-5.

18. Quoted in Mukherjee, *Education for Fulness*, p. 355.

nervous activity of youth did not discourage Tagore, for he saw it as a sign of spontaneous development:

> I would allow all our boys and girls during class to jump up, even to climb into a tree, to run off and chase after a cat or dog, or to pick some fruit off a branch...A boy would say to me, 'May I go for a run?' 'Yes, of course,' I would say, because I knew that by this means some tedium would be broken. . .[19]

Yet the environment Tagore created was adopted to impart strength and discipline. His school was simple and primitive much like any Indian *āśram*. It had only the barest of furniture, of materials and comforts, because he tried to direct the mind and spirit of the children outward to experience the world. The simplicity of the institution was a training in the acquisition of self-reliance and a hardy spirit. A type of solitude away from urban habitation and distraction was present. Recognizing the need for silence even in the life of a youth, Tagore would begin and end each day with a fifteen-minute meditation for the students. His basic conception of *brahmācārya* which he tried to inculcate among the young, was a life of discipline whereby both enjoyment and renunciation would come with ease to a resolute youth. Traditionally *brahmācārya* was the period of student life, a time for discipline, celibacy and education. Tagore saw it as a moment for the disciplining of youth against premature gratifications, and his *āśram* school provided the right kind of environment for it.

A significant aspect of his school was its communal context. The school was based on the family system where group cooperation was paramount. Tagore believed that education should be the common creation of teachers, organizers and students. Inherent in the educative process was the establishment of communion between man and nature. Education is "to know man and to make oneself known to man."[20] It should not be removed from the life current of the people. The

19. *Ibid.*, p. 363.

20. Quoted in "Rabindranath as an Educationist," Hirendranath Datta, *Rabindranath Tagore, Homage from Visva-Bharati*, p. 153.

communal nature of the *āśram* school brought people in contact with one another whereby the meeting of minds and spirits gave birth to a joy: "This joy is creative and the education imparted in the *āśram* should be instinctive with this joy."[21] The activity principle was advocated in education but activity with social significance. A national education, according to Tagore, must grow out of the social needs of the people and ultimately harmonize with world-wide fellowship. Knowledge must bring one to a consciousness of human unity. Thus the school was in no way separated from ordinary daily life in society. In fact Tagore was most impressed by the education he had observed in visits to Russia because there the boundary of the school encompassed full social life. He never ceased to stress the communal nature of education because he realized that the spiritual unity of man is achieved through both nature and neighbour.

Tagore's educational environment, natural, open, free and communal, was the primary means to evoke imagination and emotions, love and knowledge for the building of the whole man.

What dissatisfied Tagore in his youth was that the "school had not the completeness of the world."[22] In speaking of Leonard Elmhirst, a British colleague at his early school, he observed that Elmhirst believed as he did in the "organic wholeness of the individual."[23] A wholistic education is realized through creative activity which elicits the aesthetic sense. Art, for Tagore, is the bridge between man and the world, since the cardinal principle in his educational theory is the freedom for creative self-expression. The poet raised the aesthetic sense to a type of reason and aesthetic emotion to the level of knowledge. Thus he was able to stress the creative and artistic aspects of learning, crafts, work and play. He considered education essentially as an art whose methodology is determined by the aesthetic imagination. His goal was not merely to create an aesthetic culture but also a vigorous and imaginative

21. Tagore, "Thoughts on Education," p. 6.

22. *Personality*, p. 123.

23. Tagore, "A Poet's School," *The Visva-Bharati Quarterly*, Vol. IV, No. 3, Oct. 1926, p. 208.

approach to study and work. His ideal was the scriptural harmony of all existence, the nourishing of the whole man, through education. For Tagore the mind is nourished in truth; the imagination is nourished in art; and the world of relationship is nourished in sympathy for the created universe. The aesthetic sense became the synthetic principle in his conception of wholistic learning.

Education for Tagore was the gradual and progressive growth of an organism. A child grows as an organism grows. Education in his school began with training of instincts and emotions and in self-reliance and communal cooperation; then art, music and play were introduced; only with this foundation was an attempt made toward intellectual understanding; the social and economic patterns of national and international culture were introduced last of all.[24] In the process growth becomes organic and wholistic. The Dalton Plan was followed in the Santiniketan schools whereby students remained in groups determined by their own progress in a subject. This also advanced a gradual and a wholistic development.

Such pedagogy called for the coordination of all cultural resources in which the harmonization of resources with the full range of human existence took place. The curriculum, for example, of Tagore's aspiration was not subject-centered but activity centered. Education *in* activity and play preceded all else, and this was followed by training *through* activity and play in order to develop a hardy youth. Tagore pursued culture in the widest sense: through art, dance, drama, music, crafts and practical skills of daily life. He, nonetheless, placed emphasis on the fine arts and literature. In an essay on "The Place of Music in Education," he encouraged educators to make it natural for people to reverence art.[25] Music and the fine arts always had a place at the centre of Indian education and were among the highest forms of national self-expression. Without these the people remained inarticulate, according to Tagore. He urged his teachers to discover how education

24. Tagore, "Education for Rural India," *The Visva-Bharati Quarterly*, Education No., Vol. XIII, Parts I & II, May-Oct. 1947, p. 31.

25. Tagore, "The Place of Music in Education and Culture," *Ibid.*, p. 45.

could be made musical in one way or another.[26] He created opportunities at Santiniketan whereby those teachers who had musical talents could exercise them and this was meant to have an unconscious effect upon the ears of the students. With an activity-centered curriculum in mind, Tagore considered drama and the expressiveness of histrionics as compulsory. Art and music, however, were meant not merely for the well educated but also for the inspiration of the villagers.

Literature was the true vehicle of education which, Tagore believed, carried it beyond schools and colleges. He encouraged the reading and knowledge of folk literature for its cultural significance and in order to grasp the psychology of the people. Tagore would frequently encourage his students to read merely books of entertainment. He made a strong plea for Bengali as the medium of education and publicly opposed the use of English in the Indian schools. When he adopted his mother tongue, Bengali, at the turn of the century, in the schools, it was considered a revolutionary move. He observed that the harmonization of education and life could only come about through one's own language. In the schools influenced by British education, he saw that much time was spent in learning the language with little opportunity for access to the underlying thought which resulted immediately in the dissociation of thought and language. Language and thought could only be brought together through the medium of one's cultural language, and this alone could assure the integration of education with the whole of life. Tagore ultimately called for a bifurcation of the language medium, whereby basic education was imparted through the mother tongue, and other languages were pursued for their literary and social importance.

An enthusiast of the peripatetic method, teaching as he walked with his students, the poet was concerned with the association between mind and body in order to establish a total rhythm and harmony in life. He believed that children must express themselves with their whole bodies and that education of the body must be in contact with air, water, earth and light. The

26. Mukherjee, p. 143.

body "should sway with the inner movement of the thought".[27] Employing the whole body, movement must accompany thought and emotions. Tagore wrote that "I tried to keep in mind the need of the child to use the whole of its body in acquiring a vocabulary and in mastering a sentence."[28] Differing from the development of the muscular and vascular and nervous systems, the expression of the wholeness of the body must be one with the personality. He believed this possible because "the body is more than this mechanism, it is divine."[29] It is a creation.

"To give spiritual culture to our boys was my principal object in starting my school at Bolpur," reflected Tagore. "This school should be a home and a temple in one where teaching should be a part of worshipful life."[30] An experience of the spiritual world, according to him, had to be gained by living in the world and not through religious or theological teaching. He considered moral instruction a waste of time and effort. Although advocating meditation for all his students, he opposed any teaching in meditation. He also opposed any teaching of world religions in the schools due to the communal factionalism existing in India. He did not approve of the inculcation of ideology. The teaching of religion takes place not through formal lessons but is assimilated where there is a living religion. He believed that artificial means of religious education abstract both religion and education. Religious education is possible only in the natural atmosphere of piety. Herein religion should be left to the instincts of the youth, for nature and culture are the vehicles of a lived spirituality. A religious atmosphere can be created. When such an atmosphere permeates a community, religious education takes place. Tagore believed that man's education had to be liberated from the physical envelopment of religion and that this liberation would

27. Tagore, "The Art of Movement in Education," quoted in Tagore & Elmhirst, *Rabindranath Tagore: Pioneer in Education*, p. 105.
28. *Ibid.*, p. 108.
29. Tagore, *Lectures and Addresses*, ed. Anthony X. Soares (London: Macmillan & Co., Ltd., 1928), p. 63.
30. Quoted in Chaturvedi, *Tagore at Santiniketan, A Survey of Rabindranath Tagore's Educational Experiments at Santiniketan*, (Bombay: Mathai's Publications, 1934), p. 38.

lead to the establishment of the spiritual bond within the community.

Tagore's educational theory is based on his experience of the child's mind. Since education is a common enterprise between student and teacher, the school becomes complete through the student. He viewed the child as a child and not as an adult, and he realized that the sub-conscious mind of a child is more vital than its active mind. Although he wanted students to "be fully conscious of their own youthfulness, conscious that they were not grown-up people," he anticipted that their creative minds would build their own words and would be free to manage their own lives.[31] They should be free to do as they wished. The child should be allowed to stumble on and be surprised at everything that happens around him. "The young mind should be saturated with the idea that it has been born into a human world which is in harmony with the world around it."[32] Observing that a child learns easily, Tagore enunciated three principles in a child's self-education: freedom, fullness and vastness.

The most important medium of human development for Tagore is the *guru-śiṣya* (teacher-student) relationship. *Guru* and student are bound together in the classical Hindu rite of initiation, *upanayana*, and it is the same intimacy of relationship that Tagore tried to recreate. In this relationship both the teacher and the student live together in natural surroundings leading the disciplined life of *brahmācārya*. The immediate and intimate relationship awakens the minds of both. They come together to learn from each other and strive to be one as both aspire to new birth and purification.

The teacher and not the method is ultimate in Tagore's educational thought. The primary function of the teacher is to produce an atmosphere for creative activity within the *āśram* school. Tagore's exemplary teacher is a leader, a pioneer "whose chief specialization is in the art of liberating individual initiative and enterprise and making the active use of the

31. Tagore, "To the Child," *The Modern Review*, Vol. XXXVII, No. 5, May 1925, p. 500.

32. *Personality*, p. 114.

freedom principle joyous and fruitful in each case."[33] He is one who can "knock on doors of mind."[34] Tagore considered that "he who has lost the child in himself is absolutely unfit for the work of educating."[35] Those fit for teaching must have a natural feeling of respect even for the very young. High-lighting the childlike character of the teacher in his educational essays, he observed that "If one is born a teacher, the primitive child in him spontaneously comes out at the call of children."[36] Reflecting upon his own experience, he recalled that "I became the playmate of my students and shared their life completely."[37] Such a teacher must accept his students as his friends. Tagore laid emphasis on this youthful capacity of the teacher because he saw him as one who is himself still in the process of learning. He considered forebearance as requisite for teaching and believed that the presence of learned men draws students together. Tagore chartered a challenging course for the teacher:

> ...only he can teach who can love. The greatest teachers of men have been lovers of men. The real teaching is a gift; it is a sacrifice; it is not a manufactured article of routine work; and because it is a living thing, it is the fulfilment of knowledge for the teacher himself.[38]

The prototype of Tagore's ideal teacher is found in his popular play *Phalguni* (The Cycle of Spring). Here the spiritual growth of man is the mark of the *guru*, and also the only measure of his success as an educator.[39] In academic teaching we discover subjects and areas of thought but frequently not the man who pursues them. Tagore gave importance not only

33. Mukherjee, p. 70. This is Mukherjee's own observation.
34. Tagore, quoted in Chaturvedi, *Tagore at Santiniketan*, p. 106.
35. Tagore, "Thoughts on Education," p. 5.
36. Tagore, quoted in Mukherjee, *Education for Fulness*, p. 176.
37. Tagore, "The Schoolmaster," *The Modern Review*, Vol. XXXVI, No. 4, May 1924, p. 371.
38. *Letters from Abroad*, p. 14.
39. Mukherjee, p. 49. Tagore is quoted "...in my school here I think it proper to measure our success by the spiritual growth of the teachers."

to the creative self-giving of the teacher but also to communication through the personality of the teacher. After meeting Sylvain Levy in Paris, Tagore observed that Levy's students loved his subject because they loved him: "I realized clearly when I met these great teachers that only through the medium of personality can truth be communicated to men."[40] He was called "The Great Sentinel" by his admirers, but his students and colleagues understood him best through his singing and acting. poetry and drama revealed his personality and his greatest moments as a teacher. At these moments he fulfilled his name, Rabindranath: Light-Bearer.

40. *Letters from Abroad*, p. 13.

CHAPTER FOUR

Praxis and Significance

A school for boys was established in Bolpur, one hundred miles north of Calcutta, on December 22, 1901, which Tagore named Santiniketan, The Abode of Peace. He called it his "tangible poem," and observed that it resembled "a work of art and not a pedagogical laboratory."[1] He began with five teachers of whom three were Christians including a Britisher. Initiated as a centre of indigenous learning and culture, Santiniketan had all the characteristics of a garden school in the midst of nature, *āśram* life, *gurukula* (a residential hermitage), and communal fraternity filled with song. Tagore supervised all the details of the school: administration, teaching, participating in the activities and writing sixteen textbooks in Bengali. The early years were difficult and authority changed hands several times with little apparent success. Many reasons have been advanced for the slow and indecisive start, from the idealism and vagueness of Tagore's goals to the divergence of opinions among the staff. There was an indefiniteness of rules and process, and possibly the poet was ready only for the role of a *guru* and not of an administrator. This, however, indicated the experimental nature of Santiniketan from its inception.

When Tagore started Santiniketan he had no experience in education and learned only through experiment with its consequent failures and successes. There existed no preconceiv-

1. Tagore, "My Educational Mission," p. 621.

ed plan, but Santiniketan grew according to its own inner logic. The educational goals were formulated gradually in those early years, but the realization of these goals soon became apparent. Santiniketan drew the interest of Madame Montessori and John Dewey, with whom Tagore discussed contemporary education, because it was a recognized centre of experimental education. And it remained an experiment because Tagore was continually developing and expanding the relationships between education and the individual, education and the community, education and the Indian renaissance, and education and the evolutionary urge of mankind. Santiniketan became a popular private and domestic school which Bengali parents found attractive for their children. They saw exemplified in it an idealism and independence from government control, visible educational reform and a lively cultural environment.

Tagore began Santiniketan with a mere sketch of what it could be. He wrote:

> At first the object in view was purely patriotic, but later on it grew more spiritual. Then, in the very midst of all these outer difficulties, i.e., establishing Santiniketan and trials, there came the greatest change of all, the true *varsha Sesha* (end of the old year), the change in my own inner life.[2]

The inner change in Tagore came through the experiences of the death of his wife, a son and a daughter. At this time he wrote the Bengali poems of *Gitanjali* for himself and not for publication. This tranformation in the poet brought to him the realization that Santiniketan was his *sādhana* (spiritual work). Thus he could write that "Santiniketan exists for manifesting the universal man."[3]

Although Santiniketan was conceived as a centre of culture and intellectual life, it grew into a social and economic centre in India which encompased the cultivation of land, the production of necessities and practical industrial training. Santiniketan

2. *Letters to a Friend*, p. 24.
3. Quoted in Mukherjee, p. 90.

grouped neighbouring villages around itself and got integrated with them in a vital way. In the course of years Tagore sought a reform of Santiniketan because it had become too public and ordinary. In the neighbouring village of Surul he established Sriniketan, The Abode of Plenty. With village reconstruction through cooperative work as its objective, Siksha-Satra was begun as a weekly boarding school for boys. Again Tagore had no concrete plan to begin with but depended upon the creativity of teachers and students and the village itself. He was assisted by Dr. Leonard K. Elmhirst and Kalimohan Ghosh. Sriniketan was to bear the first fruits of Tagore's international collaboration, since it had on its staff Elmhirst from England, Gretchen Green and Dr. Harry Timbers from the United States of America and Kasahara from Japan. In time Sriniketan had developed cooperative health societies and storehouses, cottage industries and village crafts. In the basic and senior school of Siksha-Satra, groups of boys from different castes were brought together in one class in order to break down caste barriers.

Tagore soon gave greater importance to Sriniketan than Santiniketan because it approached closer to his ideals than his first school. At Santiniketan he had to compromise his ideals, but at Sriniketan he tried to introduce methods which he considered absolutely necessary for good education. He told Elmhirst that "You know my heart is with Surul. I feel that it has life in it—it does not deal with abstractions, but has its roots deep in the heart of living reality."[4] Out of Siksha-Satra came Tagore's idea of an education basic to the needs of rural society. The immediate goals were the development of self-respect and intelligent self-help. These could be achieved, he believed, if education emerged from the village itself, that is, if the teacher and the student learned directly from the village and carried on their creative work within the village. Tagore brought his social thought especially to Sriniketan for he always gave the highest point to rural uplift and reconstruction. Yet his goal was the unification of both spiritual and social man. Village service must begin out of respect for village life and not out of condescension. The

4. Tagore & Elmhirst, *A Pioneer in Education*, p. 37.

creative activity of the village was to be as important as its economic life. Awakening a sense of service within the village Tagore believed, could develop self-determination and cooperation among the castes. Reflecting upon the establishment of Sriniketan some years later, Tagore said, "My aim has been to assist in bringing the flood-tide of life's joy to the arid villages, urging them towards diverse self-expression."[5] His scope was not necessarily wide, but he believed that if he could "free one or two villages from the bonds of ignorance and weakness, there will be built, on a tiny scale, an ideal for the whole of India."[6] He was convinced that the villages possessed the potential for creative life.

The apex of Tagore's educational endeavours came with the founding of a university at Santiniketan. Following upon his restlessness to expand the *āśram* school, his thought and praxis now extended to universal fullness and international education. He laid the cornerstone of Visva-Bharati in 1918, and on December 23, 1921, it was formally approved by the Government of Bengal and inaugurated. Ten years after his death, in 1951, it was raised to a national university. The name, Visva-Bharati, indicates the vision which gave birth to it. *Visva* is Sanskrit for universe or world; *Bharati* can either mean the goddess of culture and learning or the Aryan name for India. Thus Visva-Bharati meaning world and India signifies Tagore's conception of a centre for universal learning. He had financial obstacles to overcome before launching the university. Although the seed for the university was in his mind a decade previous to its foundation, he spent much time and energy in advancing and evolving the concept of international education, before it took shape.

Yatra viśvaṃ bhavaty eka-nīḍam is the Sanskrit motto of Visva-Bharati: "Where the universe has become a single nest." The motto selected by Tagore indicates his primary vision: humanity, universal man, in totality and universality. He sought in Visva-Bharati a common fellowship of learning and

5. Tagore, "Sriniketan, *The Visva-Bharati News*, Vol. VII, No. 8, Feb. 1939.
6. Quoted in Naravane, "Tagore and the Middle Path," *The Century Book of Tagore*, ed. Sookamal Ghose (Calcutta: Granthan, Prakash Chandra Saha, 1961), p. 90.

a common spiritual striving that would be truly international and that would bring East and West face to face. He envisioned an academic community with no geographical boundaries, a community experiencing universality. He perceived this moment in history as opportune : "The peoples have come together . . . we must establish relations with this truth." Education must be freed from its nationalism for "Tomorrow is to begin the chapter of the federation of races."[7] He projected nothing less than the spiritual unity of all races, a universal brotherhood, a place for those who believed in the spiritual unity of races and those who have suffered from a lack of it. He wanted the university to be a place where the different peoples and cultures could reveal themselves to one another and then to find ground for common interests which would result in understanding and reconciliation.

The university initially consisted of four divisions: higher secondary, college, research and rural education. Tagore did not envision just another Indian university. He intended first to establish an Eastern university, a centre of culture for the Aryan, Christian, Semitic, Mongolian, Chinese and Japanese heritages. Several of his lengthy visits to China and Japan were attempts to call forth an Asian movement for cooperation in education. He urged the Chinese and Japanese to join with India in the harmonization of Asian culture and spirituality. He saw in an Eastern centre of culture the possibility of intellectual cooperation and collaboration. In short he sought a synthesis of Asian culture, and Visva-Bharati was where the Asian mind could be reflected to the rest of the world. The most comprehensive notion that Tagore had of Visva-Bharati was that of a meeting place between the Asian culture and the West.

Visva-Bharati probably brought greater anguish to Tagore than any other endeavour because of the conflict of interests and ideals that prevailed among his colleagues. At times the university drifted. Efforts were made to consolidate Indian culture through a free interchange of scholars and to relate education more directly to the people. The university tried to coordinate

7. Tagore "The Union of Cultures," *The Modern Review*, Vol. XXX, No. 5, Nov. 1921, p. 541.

the study of the different Indian cultures i.e. Vedic, Puranic, Buddhist, Jain, Islamic, Sikh and Zoroastrian. It had a distinctive Indian character which was still international. Tagore did not want the Indian personality lost at Visva-Bharati, but he strove to bring the diverse minds of India into some coordinated activity. Although he was not able to draw large numbers of Far Eastern scholars to Visva-Bharati, some beginnings were made in this direction.

The broad humanism that Tagore anticipated for the university is articulated in the "Aims and Objects of Visva-Bharati," contained in the University Prospectus even today:

> To study the mind of Man in its realization of different aspects of truth from diverse points of view.
> To bring into more intimate relation with one another, through patient study and research, the different cultures of the East on the basis of their underlying unity.
> To approach the West from the standpoint of such a unity of the life and thought of Asia.
> To seek to realize in a common fellowship of study the meeting of the East and the West, and thus ultimately to strengthen the fundamental conditions of world peace through the establishment of free communication of ideas between the two hemispheres.
> And with such ideals in view to provide at Santiniketan a centre of culture where research into and study of the religion, literature, history, science and art of Hindu, Buddhist, Jain, Islamic, Sikh, Christian and other civilizations may be pursued along with the culture of the West, with that simplicity in externals which is necessary for true spiritual realization, in amity, good fellowship and cooperation between thinkers and scholars of both Eastern and Western countries, free from all antagonisms of race, nationality, creed or caste.

This manifesto of acadamic liberation has not yet been realized at Santiniketan. However, Tagore's dream to make an Indian a citizen of the world achieved fulfilment in his own personality. He experienced that "East and West meet in friendship in my own person." He had hoped to bring the East and the West into reconciliation because he had perceived that "we are complimentary."[8] Visva-Bharati as an international centre was based on a philosophy of education which sought universality. It reflects again the poet's basic philosophy of man, as one who thirsts for universality. A key factor in his philosophy, as the creation of Visva-Bharati indicated, was the eventual reconciliation of things through more universal experience.

Writing to Gilbert Murray during the critical period following the First World War, Tagore remarked that he had no solutions for the problems of the world other than the educational colony of Santiniketan. He considered this community within nature, a place of freedom for self-expression and international vision, as unique. Those who had observed Santiniketan from its inception saw the humanization of Indian education as its major contribution. Since Santiniketan emerged from the poet's experiences and experiments with all of life, he evolved not necessarily a new system of education but a new pattern of life, joyful and free, within education. Tagore's legacy is the view that education is always developing, an emergent creation, ever-evolving toward universal man. The success of Santiniketan cannot be measured by external achievements but by the opportunity it gives for human growth. His emphasis on the aesthetic and nature and the meeting of the East and the West were means to establish this opportunity. His interest in comparative study, based upon a complimentarity of cultures, was the keynote of the coming age because he viewed the different civilizations expressing different aspects of truth. "The past has been for men, the future is for Man," epitomised Tagore's achievement as a humanistic educator.[9]

Negative criticism of Tagore's experiment focused upon the *āśram* idealism, the formation of effete as against rigorous students, and the repetition of spiritual values which pervaded his theory and praxis. Tagore confronted these criticisms throughout his life. Sasadhar Sinha has made the sharpest criticism of Santiniketan in contemporary times. He believes that Tagore generalized excessively by making normative the

8. Tagore quoted in Suryanarayana, *Tagore as Educationist*, p. 7.

9. *Letters to a Friend*, p. 104.

results of his own experiences which were based on an extraordinary mind and a very special education and family life. The poet, Sinha claims, was not able to draw about him a body of intellectuals who could share his vision and the responsibilities of Santiniketan. Sinha does not view Santiniketan today very positively because it had changed considerably from the time of its conception. It has produced, he thinks, neither the intellectually vigorous nor has it offered a broad and balanced intellectual discipline. Yet Santiniketan is a success, according to Sinha, as an educational experiment and as the accumulation of a body of Tagorean traditions. Whether Visva-Bharati is primarily a university or a research centre, likewise, seems unresolved to Sinha. Since it became a national university in 1951, Sinha observes that changes in administration and in the physical structure have not influenced its academic life.[10] Stephen Hay in a major work on Tagore's influence in Asia has based Visva-Bharati's shortcomings on Tagore's faulty thesis of an East-West synthesis. Hay's research has shown that Tagore could not convince East Asians of a cultural synthesis within Asia itself.[11] H.B. Mukherjee, in the most definitive study on Tagore's educational work, detected upon visits to Santiniketan in 1940 and again in 1958 a drift towards formalism and mechanization and, of course, the transformation of Santiniketan into a town and not the country school of the poet's time.[12] Yet Mukherjee and Humayun Kabir, both contemporary Indian educationists, unreservedly believe that all educational ideals in India for the past half century have drawn upon the Santiniketan experiment.[13] There are Santiniketan-type schools throughout India. Kabir concludes that Tagore's insights are still very much in effect in Santiniketan because of its visible touch with Indian culture and community life.[14] Following recent student and faculty dissatisfaction,

10. Sinha, *The Social Thinking of Rabindranath Tagore*, pp. 79-92.
11. Stephen N. Hay, *Asian Ideas of East and West* (Boston: Harvard University Press, 1970).
12. Mukherjee, p. 452.
13. Humayun Kabir, *Education in New India*, (London: George Allen & Unwin, 1956),p. 52
14. Humayun Kabir, *Indian Philosophy of Education* (Bombay: Asia Publishing House, 1961), p. 46.

the Masud Committee submitted a report in December 1975 to improve the standards of Visva-Bharati. The impression a visitor to Santiniketan will have today is the existence of a close-knit community of academicians, on the one hand, and the visible concern for rural development at Sriniketan on the other. The simplicity of the institution in its rural and natural surroundings still distinguishes it from most Indian universities.

Santiniketan and other institutions for that matter can only imitate the poet's dream outwardly because the uniqueness lies within the personality of Tagore. His greatest gift was the gift of his personality. He saw the building of Santiniketan "as the divine humanity working in his mind and compelling him to practical activities."[15] The history of Santiniketan is the history of his own spiritual voyage. The personality of the poet reflected a divine humanity which inspired both students and colleagues. Rabindranath, which means the essence of the day's light, taught through the light of his own personality. And this light was the medium of truth and inspiration of Santiniketan. He wrote that "I believe this material world is built on light; that matter, in its ultimate stage, is Light."[16] The symbolism of light is frequent in his poetry. Yet Tagore always felt an ambivalence as educator for he sensed "that poets should never bind themselves to any particular work; for they are the instruments of the world's moods."[17] Nonetheless, Tagore's personality reflected his conception of the educative process as an effective harmony of relationships and growth of total personality through relationships.[18]

15. *The Religion of Man*, p. 160.
16. *Thoughts from Rabindranath Tagore*, p. 185.
17. *Letters to a Friend*, p. 60.
18. Sarkar, *Tagore's Educational Philosophy and Experiment*, p. 40.

PART TWO

MOHANDAS K. GANDHI

1869-1948

CHAPTER FIVE

The Man: The Experimental Personality

Gandhi was not a revolutionary personality by birth. His career of non-violence emerged from his personal experience in private and public life. Dedication to the social welfare of the nation was a gradual commitment for him which ultimately developed into a religion of service. Gandhi had the gift to learn and grow within ordinary experiences and experimentation with the events of daily life and the principles he gradually evolved drew him closer to a comprehensive life of non-violence.

Mohandas Karamchand Gandhi was born on October 2, 1869, in Porbandar, a seacoast town of Gujarat. His family belonged to the Bania caste and its members were originally grocers, but his father and grandfather had become prime ministers in the Kathiawar district. They were traditional Vaiṣṇāvas and his mother, Putlibai, made a strong impression upon young Mohandas with her piety and common-sense. She went daily to the Vaiṣṇāva temple, fasted frequently, took numerous vows, and was sought out for her practical wisdom. Mohandas was a shy youth, aloof, weak in health and he possessed a nervous temperament. He was a mediocre student showing no great capacities and spent much of his youth nursing his ailing father. As a result of this a strong relationship grew between them. Besides, nursing became a lifelong interest for him.

In his autobiography Gandhi looked upon his life as a series of experiments with truth and concluded that "life consists in nothing but those experiments."[1] The young Mohandas was betrothed three times before he married Kasturbai at the age of thirteen. He spoke of "playing the husband"[2] in an attempt to educate his young wife, and he entered boyhood friendships "in the spirit of a reformer."[3] During his high school years, he violated family customs by eating meat and smoking. To support his smoking habit, he along with a young friend resorted to stealing, but Mohandas finally resolved to confess the failing to his father in writing. The incident left a lasting mark upon him for his father was completely forgiving, and Gandhi recalled the experience as his first lesson in receiving pure *ahiṃsa* (non-violence) from another.[4]

From his nurse, Rambha, he learned to repeat the name of Rāma but had no strong affection for the Vaiṣṇāva tradition. The family exhibited a broad religious toleration by visiting not only the Heveli temple of the Vaiṣṇāvas but also those of Śiva and Rāma. Jain monks, Muslim and Parsi friends were frequent visitors in their home. The first of his four sons was born in 1888, the year that he left for England to begin studies tn law. Before departing he vowed to his mother that he would not touch wine, women or meat, since he was to leave Kasturbai, his wife, and son in India. It was against the rules of his caste

1. Mohandas K. Gandhi, *An Autobiography, The Story of my Experiments with Truth*, trans. Mahadev Desai (Boston : Beacon Press, 1956), p. xii. Biographies of Gandhi are numerous and of varied quality. A comprehensive work but neither selective nor definitive is the eight volume *Mahatma : Life of M.K. Gandhi,* Dinanath Gopal Tendulkar (Bombay: Jhaveri & Tendulkar, 1951-54). *Mahatma Gandhi : The Last Phase* (Ahmedabad: Navajivan Press, 1956-58) is necessary for the last years, written by Pyarelal Nayar, a close associate of Gandhi. Biographies by Romain Rolland, Vincent Sheean, Henry L. S. Polak, George Catlin, Bal Ram Nanda, P.C. Ghosh, Ela Sen and Chandra Shukla are informative. Louis Fischer's *The Life of Mahatma Gandhi* (New York: Harper & Bros., 1950) and *Gandhi* (New York: Stein & Day, 1968) by Geoffrey Ashe by two Western biographers are well done. Jawaharlal Nehru's, *Mahatma Gandhi* (Bombay & New York : Asia Publishing House, 1965) is also perceptive.
2. Gandhi, *An Autobiography*, pp. 11-14.
3. *Ibid.*, p. 19.
4. *Ibid.*, pp. 27-28.

to go abroad, and the caste formally excommunicated him before he left.

England was a liberating experince for the nineteen-year old youth. In his three years in London, he confronted for the first time the social and revolutionary theories prevalent in Europe, an impressive body of Western literature, and Western people interested in Indian religious traditions. He read with seriousness scriptures of the world and contemporary social theories for the first time. His first reading of the *Bhagavad Gītā* in 1889 was Sir Edwin Arnold's translation, *The Song Celestial.* He met Theosophists, Christians and Quakers and read Blavatsky's *Key to Theosophy* after meeting both Madame Blavatsky and Annie Besant. He followed Kropotkin's *Mutual Aid* which was then appearing serially in a London journal. Becoming a vegetarian for dietetic reasons, Mohandas was elected to the executive committee of the London Vegetarian Society. He tried to become the English gentleman by dressing in well-tailored suits and even by taking dancing lessons. But it was in England that the young Gandhi began his life of introspection. Speaking of his personal experimentation at this time, he wrote:

> As I searched myself deeper, the necessity for change both internal and external began to grow on me. As soon as, or even before, I made alterations in my expenses and my way of life, I began to make changes in my diet.[5]

He passed the bar examination with ease and returned to India and his family in 1891, attempting to practice law but with little success. Seeing no promise for a career in India, he accepted a post as a legal counsel in South Africa. Except for brief visits to India and England, he lived in South Africa for the next twenty-one years. He found himself negotiating settlements among conflicting parties in order to avoid litigations. Gandhi first suffered severe humiliation and physical rebuke because of colour prejudice in South Africa which aroused his instinct to protest against the standing political and social orders. Discrimination and the denial of human rights to the Indian community of Natal encouraged him to enroll as an

5. *Ibid.*, p. 55.

advocate of the Natal courts, the only Indian to do so. He started with a petition to the legistative assembly which sought greater civil rights for the Indians. The Natal Indian Congress was soon formed and Gandhi became its first secretary. He viewed his legal work as secondary to the public service he rendered to the South African Indians. In 1896 he gained international attention with the famous "Green Pamphlet", *The Grievances of the British Indians in South Africa.*

A second period of introspection began and his life took on a new simplicity and asceticism. He abandoned Western dress and in 1906 took the vow of chastity. Christian and Quaker friends introduced him to the literature of non-violence. Experimentation began gradually in family life, in his legal work and in public confrontation with discrimination. Gandhi supervised the education of his wife and children and even the other members of his household. He began to develop visible ascetical habits.

A significant body of non-Indian literature had a profound effect on him during these years: for example, The Sermon on the Mount from the *New Testament*, John Ruskin's *Unto this Last*, Thoreau's *Civil Disobedience*, Leo Tolstoy's *The Kingdom of God is within You* and Emerson's essays. Whole phrases and basic terminology used by Tolstoy became part of Gandhi's spiritual and political vocabulary. Tolstoy, more than any other single influence outside of Hinduism, taught Gandhi the importance of manual work, the religious basis of non-violence, the law of love, an abhorrence for centralized government and industrialization, and the brotherhood of man. But if Tolstoy was the most important Westerner to influence Gandhi ideologically, it was left to John Ruskin to move him in the experiential order to a life of total dedication. Ruskin's call for men to die for their profession, to value only that which leads to greater life, to reach out for the maximum of virtue, courage, and love, instilled in Gandhi a pursuit of non-violence in his personal life and in the life of the South African Indian community. In organizing the South African Indians, the possibilities of non-violence loomed before him, and he launched a lifelong experimentation within himself and his followers in the methods and the spirituality of non-violence.

He established a weekly journal, *Indian Opinion*, as his literary output steadily began to increase. Civil disobedience was begun against prejudicial law; prison and assault were openly courted; suffering without retaliation was accepted. Gandhi rallied the Indian community and led massive marches of protest. Jail-going became common and at one time twenty-five hundred Indians of Transvaal were in prison. The most impressive act of protest involved fifty thousand indentured labourers striking simultaneously. The non-violent campaign reached a climax in 1913 with the 'Great March' which ended in an agreement between Gandhi and General Smuts in 1914, resulting in the Indian Relief Act. A major factor in Gandhi's conditioning for a life of non-violence was his twenty-one year long experience in South Africa. Non-violence was both discovered and developed by him there. He had rallied men to a point where ill-feeling, hatred and vindictiveness were absent in public protest. The experience revealed the creative and experimental personality of Gandhi at its best and produced an invaluable tool for later life.

Gandhi's revolutionary mainfesto, *Hind Swarāj* (Indian Home Rule), written in 1909, became the theoretical basis for future thought on society, politics, non-violence, modern civilization and the place of religion in human life. It was a revolutionary document because it sought immediate change of the present social and political order. He stated: "We shall get nothing by asking; we shall have to take what we want, and we need the requisite strength for the effort and that strength will be available to him only who acts thus."[6] This statement was followed by eighteen points of change which had to take place. However, the changes called for were centered in the life of the individual Indian. If India was to change, each Indian had to change first. The method of change was self-rule and non-violence. Freedom, from the very beginning of Gandhi's thought, was the ability to rule oneself. In *Hind Swarāj* he dedicated his life to freedom and entered into the national arena as a revolutionary personality.

6. M. K. Gandhi, *The Collected Works of Mahatma Gandhi*, (New Delhi: Publications Division, 1963) Vol. 10, *Hind Swaraj*; p. 63.

Although Gandhi was not the first in the East or the West to suggest non-violence as a means of protest and change, he was the first to place it on a comprehensive scale. Tilak in India had suggested passive resistance, government boycott, and human suffering to counteract British oppression; however, they were mere political tactics for him. Gandhi arrived in India in 1915 at the time Tilak and the extremists had reached a peak of power. Upon his return he founded the Satyāgraha Āshram and the first non-violent campaign in India under his direction soon followed with disciples trained in his *āśram*. India slowly awakened to the personality of Mohandas Gandhi. In the next thirty years he inspired, organized and led three all-India campaigns of civil disobedience against the British. The first began in 1919 against the Rowlatt Act when he called a nationwide strike (*hartal*) for one day.

In the history of non-violence Gandhi stood at the crossroads of nineteenth century social criticism and modern Indian movements. The two trends in social criticism which appealed to him were the moral equivalent school which attempted to transfer chivalric virtue to peaceful ends, and the peace movement of absolute pacifism which categorically rejected violence. Carlyle, Emerson and Ruskin represented the first school, and the Quakers and the later writings of Tolstoy represented the second, a type of pacifism which took on a negative quality. Gandhi's concept of non-violence evolved as a workable alternative to these two positions. In experimentation he forged a path between the two positions, avoiding the idealism of the one and the negativity of the other.

What had previously been implicit in the Indian conscience became explicit in the twentieth century as new movements arose. The founding of the Congress Party in 1885 by Westernized Indian intellectuals was the turning point in the history of modern India. Gopal Krishna Gokhale in establishing the Servants of India Society, committed himself and his followers in training men devoted to the cause of the country in a religious spirit. He was the political leader of the Congress Party as it entered the twentieth century, and one who believed strongly in the benevolence of the British Viceroys and the justice they would bring. Gandhi was to refer to Gokhale as his political *guru*, though the only noticeable influence was a sense of moderation and a religious commitment to moral change. A new type of nationalism, militant and rooted in Hindu orthodoxy, arose at the turn of the century under the intellectual leadership of Aurobindo Ghose and the political direction of Bal Gangadhar Tilak. This movement incited political agitation among the masses and captivated the nationalist mind. Tilak was the first to bring politics to the street and the market. He was the first political leader of modern India to identify himself with the masses, and he brought a religious fervour to politics comparable only to that of Gandhi some years later. For the first time sacrifice and suffering, experienced in prison and in political suppression, became a badge of honour and distinction among Indians. Tilak in a speeeh in 1907 suggested passive resistance and boycott to the Indian people. He sealed his leadership in 1916 by an alliance with the Muslim League called the Lucknow Pact. However, Gokhale died in 1915 and Tilak died on the very day Gandhi began his first all-India campaign. Gandhi accepted theoretically the moderation of Gokhale as also his political mantle as head of the Congress Party, but from Tilak he took the religious fervour and identification with the masses which ultimately established him as the major political leader of modern India. He belonged to the moderates but became in fact the successor of Tilak.

Gandhi was elected president of the All-India Home Rule League in 1920 and pledged to achieve *swarāj* (home-rule) in one year. A year later he was invested with executive authority by the Congress Party. Gandhi was soon jailed and he served two years of a six year sentence; while in prison he wrote his autobiography, *The Story of my Experiments with Truth*. He began public fasting against communal rioting and this became a pattern occurring intermittently throughout his life. During the 1920s Gandhi wrote his most definitive articles on non-violence, the British and independence, social reform, and religion and the spiritual life. The study of Gandhi is complicated by the vast amount of literature produced by him. Although he wrote only four works of book length, *The Story of my Experiments with Truth*, *Satyāgraha in South Africa*, *Hind Swaraj*, and *Key to Health*, the rest of his writing included speeches, articles, pamphlets and weekly newspaper pieces for *Indian Opinion*, *Young India* and *Harijan*. Gandhi's writing is still in the process of being collected and edited and when eompleted will comprise close to seventyfive volumes.

Yet he was most at ease in the simplicity of his *āśram*, spinning, experimenting with nature cures, and instructing his followers in ascetical and spiritual discipline. He wrote in *Young India* in 1919 that "*Satyāgraha* presupposes self-control, self-purification, and a recognized social status in the person offering it."[7] This summarized the rationale behind ascetical training and *āśram* life. He advocated eleven ascetical vows in his *āśram*: truth, *ahiṃsā* (non-violence), chastity, non-possession, fearlessness, control of the palate, non-stealing, bread-labour, equality of religions, anti-untouchability, and *swadeshi* (the use and production of home-made products). Only internal purification, Gandhi believed, would liberate the individual for gradual self-realization and for the work of the social community to which one belonged. The Gandhian *āśram* differed somewhat from the traditional Indian *āśram* for it strove to achieve the social ideals which Gandhi cherished.[8] It was a testing field for public protest, a mirror for all India in which to see the good society which Gandhi theorized about in his teaching and writing. It exemplified that he practised what he taught: namely, a non-violent society was a real possibility even though on a miniature scale.

On March 12, 1930, the second all-India campaign began with the historic Salt March to the sea. With seventy-eight co-workers he walked the dirty roads of India from village to village, two hundred miles in twenty-four days. His small group had grown to several thousand when, on April 5, he reached the sea. Walking along the shore he scooped up some salt remains from the beach. With this action he broke the British law which made it a crime to possess salt not obtained from the British salt monopoly. India received its cue from Gandhi. Along the vast coastline

7. M. K. Gandhi, *Satyagraha, Non-Violent Resistance*, edited., Bharatan Kumarappa (Ahmedabad: Navajivan Press, 1951), p. 77; also published as *Non-Violent Resistance, Satyagraha*, (New York: Schocken Books, 1961) with same pagination.
8. See M. K. Gandhi, *Ashram Observances in Action*, trans. Valji G. Desai (Ahmedabad: Navajivan Press, 1955).

of India thousands entered the sea with pans to make salt. Over one hundred thousand people were arrested for civil disobedience, The results of the Salt March were momentous for in spirit India had gained her freedom. The people were now convinced that they were strong enough eventually to get rid of British rule, and Britain and the world became suddenly aware of Indian subjugation.

Gandhi entered into a lengthy period during the 1930's in which he gave himself principally to constructive programmes for social improvement. He began to campaign against untouchability, and initiated the first 'fast unto death' in protest against British action which granted a separate electorate to untouchables He started another weekly journal called *Harijan* (Children of God), the name he gave to the untouchables. In 1933 he toured India for ten months to rouse public opinion against customs prejudicial to the untouchables and to bring about legislation outlawing these customs. He also devoted himself to promoting the spinning wheel and the use of Indian cloth in order to develop the spirit of self-help. Programmes in education and for the relief of the outcastes and the establishment of Hindi as a national language were intensified. During this period Gandhi formulated his educational theory more clearly and began to introduce it upon the national scene as basic education. He formally retired from the Congress Party, and Nehru became the political spokesman for India. Yet the stream of politicians to Gandhi's *āśram* was not abated in their need for leadership. As he grew older, Gandhi's experiments in the ascetical order increased and his writing grew more devotional than previously.

Although self-realization is the goal of Hinduism, it is unattainable in both Gandhi's philosophy and personal asceticism. "To develop the spirit is to build character and to enable one to work *towards* a knowledge of God and self-realization," wrote Gandhi.[9] Man tends towards perfection and self-realization, but the attainment is markedly absent from Gandhi's experience and thought. His spirituality is eminently pragmatic for man does not transcend the human condition. Devotion was not absent from his personal life, but it was not always

9. Gandhi, *An Autobiography*, p. 338.

evident in the same degree. There was a transition from an earlier emphasis of *karma-yoga* (the path of activity) to *bhakti-yoga* (the path of devotion). During his years in South Africa, Gandhi was the epitome of the *karma-yogin*; the next twenty-five years in India saw a correlation of *karma-yoga* and *bhakti-yoga*. This was the most productive period of his life. In the last ten years of his life, however, he turned more intensively towards devotionalism. This is reflected both in his writings and in his remarkably poor grasp of the political situation during these years. The more he immersed himself in the scriptures of the world the greater became his devotionalism. As he returned to the *Īśopaniṣad* and the *Bhagavad Gītā*, the foundations of scriptural Hinduism for him, the religion of service which he had conceived of early in his career led inevitably to a richer communion with God and a more profound identification with the masses. His devotional life deepened, until in the final years it was difficult to distinguish service from devotion in his daily activity.

In 1940 Gandhi permitted individual civil disobedience against the British war effort, but in August 1942 the Congress Party passed the 'Quit India' resolution calling for nationwide civil disobedience against the British. Gandhi had less influence upon the Congress Party as independence neared, but he held the affection of the masses to the very end. Several of these final years were spent in prison, and his wife Kasturbai died in prison in 1944. India finally gained political freedom in 1947, but the cost was partition on the basis of the two-nation theory. This was a blow which Gandhi did not accept and from which he never fully recovered. He had given a lifetime urging communal unity but in the end all seemed a failure. The animosity between Muslims and Hindus intensified and Gandhi toured India, frequently alone and on foot, from village to village trying to quell the rioting and killing. The final days were dark for Gandhi. He began his last fast as a result of communal factionalism and called it an 'all-in-fast,' placing the spiritual energy of eighty years into it. It was undertaken in the Delhi home of a Muslim, but peace was restored after ten days and Gandhi ended his last fast.

The Mahatma (Great Soul), the name given to Gandhi upon his political rise in India by Rabindranath Tagore, denied

Gandhism in any sectarian sense. He said, "I myself do not know what is a Gandhian hue. I am sailing an uncharted sea."[10] The experimental nature of his life was apparent to him. He struggled in the final years to discover some key to communal unity between Hindus and Muslims. He did not find such a key and became moody and depressed. Although he never realised his vision to bring about the spiritual transformation of India, he succeeded in attaining a high degree of transformation in himself and in the lives of his immediate followers. It is generally agreed that whatever Gandhi gained in India was achieved with a mixture of non-violence and violence. This was due, according to the Mahatma, to the fact that the majority who practised non-violence used it only as a tactic for political liberation and not as a pattern of life for total human transformation. This indicates the experimental and, consequently, problematic nature of non-violence itself. Gandhi's life is a testimony that human transformation is possible through a life-process of experimentation in day-to-day activity.

On January 30, 1948, in the seventy-eighth year of his life, Gandhi was shot by Vinayak N. Godse, a Hindu fanatic as he was walking to an evening prayer meeting at Birla House in Delhi. He died murmuring, "Hey Ram" (Oh, God). Jawaharlal Nehru, his political successor, announced to the nation his death: "A glory has departed. The sun that warmed and brightened our lives has set, and we shiver in the cold and the dark."[11] Upon later reflection Pandit Nehru, now leading the new nation, said of the Mahatma:

> He seems to be the vehicle and embodiment of some greater force of which even he is perhaps only dimly conscious. Is that the spirit of India, the accumulated spirit of the millennia that lie behind our race, the memory of a thousand tortured lives ?[12]

10. M. K. Gandhi, *The Mind of Mahatma Gandhi*, comp. & edit. R. K. Prabhu & U. R. Rao (Ahmedabad: Navajivan Press, 1945), p. 26.
11. Jawaharlal Nehru, *Nehru on Gandhi* (New York: Signet Press), p. 154, quoted in V.S. Naravane, *Modern Indian Thought* (Bombay & New York: Asia Publishing House, 1964), p. 168.
12. Ibid., quoted in Naravane, *Modern Indian Thought*, p. 169.

CHAPTER SIX

His Thought: Karma Yoga

Gandhi involved himself in causes other than political liberation, for example, the social and ethical education of the people, the removal of untouchability, the abolition of child marriages, the equality of women and village reforms. Although meaningful, these causes did not constitute his basic motivation. The commitment to a cause was secondary to the more fundamental dedication to the people. "Cause without the people is a dead thing. Love of the people brought the problem of untouchability early into my life," reflected Gandhi.[1] He raised his dedication to the people to a religion of service and, there-

1. M. K. Gandhi, *Non-Violence in Peace and War*, edit. Bharatan Kumarappa (Ahmedabad: Navajivan Press, 1942), Vol. 1, p. 182. I have found the following philosophical studies useful for this study: Joan V. Bondurant, *Conquest of Violence, The Gandhian Philosophy of Conflict* (Berkeley: University of California, rev. edit., 1965) ; Dhirendra Mohan Datta, *The Philosophy of Mahatma Gandhi* (Madison, Wisconsin:University of Wisconsin, 1953) ; H. J. N. Horsburgh, *Non-Violence and Aggression, A Study of Gandhi's Moral Equivalent of War* (London: Oxford University Press, 1968) ; Simone Panter-Brick, *Gandhi against Machiavellism, Non-Violence in Politics* (London: Asia Publishing House, 1966) ; James Weldon Plaugher, "The Religious Aspects of Gandhi's Ahimsa," Ph.D. unpub. diss., Stanford University, 1965; Rama Chandran & Mahadevan, editors, *Gandhi: His Relevance for our Times* (New Delhi: Gandhi Peace Foundation, 1967); Indira Rothermund, *The Philosophy of Restraint* (Bombay: Popular Prakashan, 1963).

after, considered his motive purely religious. The particular inspiration that Hinduism gave him was through the classical *Bhagavad Gītā*; he considered the second and third chapters of the *Gītā* as the core of Hinduism. These chapters specifically discuss the life of *karma-yoga* (the discipline of activity) and form the theoretical basis for a religion of service. The *Gītā* gave him the much needed motivation for a religious dedication to the service of man.

A *karma-yogin*, according to the *Gītā*, does not separate religious life from an active role in society. Gandhi, likewise, did not sever the two: "You cannot divide social, economic, political and purely religious work into watertight compartments. I do not know any religion apart from human activity."[2] The continuity between religious life and secular activity is a common Indian perception which calls for the integration of all life with the Supreme. In his commentary on the *Gītā*, Gandhi wrote: "Action takes its origin from the Imperishable Brahma; therefore the Imperishable Brahma is present in all kinds of sacrifice of service."[3] Gandhi's activism was consistent with the Hindu tradition which considered all life sacred. Since society and social work are integral to life, they are inherently sacred activities. An identity with all that lives includes dedication to the welfare of man. Gandhi's religion of service was based upon a profound commitment to the Indian people, and in this commitment the *karma-yogin* achieved self-realization. "For me the road to salvation lies through incessant toil in the service of my country and therefore of humanity," he wrote. "My patriotism is a stage in my journey to the land of eternal freedom and peace."[4]

Gandhi followed strictly the teaching of the *Gītā* in resolving the ascetical dilemma whether to enter into the life of the world or to withdraw from it. Kṛṣṇa, in the *Gītā*, tells Arjuna to continue his duty (*svadharma*) but to renounce the fruits of his actions and accomplishments. Detachment from action even

2. *Non-Violence in Peace and War*, Vol.1, p. 182.
3. M. K. Gandhi, *Gita My Mother*, edit. Anand T. Hingorani (Bombay: Bharatiya Vidya Bhavan, 1965), p. 148.
4. M. K. Gandhi, *Hindu Dharma*. (Ahmedabad: Navajivan Publishing House, 1950), p. 13.

while engulfed in acton became a distinctive factor in Gandhi's philosophy. In religious terms it meant renunciation, and when renunciation of the fruits of activity was integral to the social personality, a spiritual rebirth took place. The activity which thus motivates the individual is selfless action, a disinterested service which seeks no personal gain. It is a pure form of altruism consisting in unreciprocated activity. Gandhi interpreted the central teaching of the *Gītā* as selfless action, non-attachment (*anaśakti*), and believed that non-violence (*ahiṃsā*) is a necessary preliminary to it and included in it. Non-attachment became for him the motivation which humanized political and social activity by keeping him above selfish interests or overly consumed by the actual goals of public service.

His life was a conscious experimentation within the particular activity in which he found himself, and the activity was raised to a religion of service, a *karma-yoga*. He possessed, however, an ambivalence in his self-concept for he could say that "The politician in me never dominated a single decision of mine," and still maintained that "Men say I am a saint losing myself in politics. The fact is I am a politician trying my hardest to be a saint."[5] Both statements embrace *karma-yoga* as a fundamental philosophy of life.

The *Gītā* speaks about the man of steady wisdom (*sthitaprajñā*) and stable spirit (*samādhistha*) who is capable of determining his own life and of acting rightly. Gandhi was concerned with norms which would stabilize social man in wisdom and action. He spoke of the man who would not fall into anger and contention but would remain unaffected by adulation or abuse. Such a man would "never wish ill to anyone, but will pray even for his enemy with his last breath. Is it too difficult to follow? No. On the contrary, the conduct laid down in it is the only conduct worthy of the dignity of human beings."[6] To create a permanent condition in man, firm in motivation and service, is the

5. M. K. Gandhi, *Satyagraha, Non-Violent Resistance*, edit. Bharatan Kumarappa (Ahmedabad: Navajivan Press, 1951), p. 109, quoted in Louis Fischer, *Gandhi, His Life and Message for the World* (New York: Mentor Books, 1954), p. 35.

6. *Gita My Mother*, p. 71.

function of truth and *ahimsā* (non-violence). Truth and non-violence are normative in human conduct and at the same time are the source from which the individual acts firmly and decisively. These norms became the core of Gandhi's ideology and the basis for activity whether spiritual, social or political.

Non-attachment to the immediate results of activity renders social acts spiritual and human. Yet Gandhi searched for the deeper roots of non-attachment, since there had to be adherence to something if the individual was to be detached from the fruits of activity but still vitally active. Such an individual attached himself unreservedly to truth and *ahimsā*. 'There is no greater law than truth' (*Satyam nāsti parmo dharmaḥ*) is a common aphorism in the Hindu tradition. The *Vedas* contain the concept of binding truth which commits the individual to *Brahman* and assures a concern for man. In the early *Vedas* and *Upaniṣads* truth (*satya*) is not strictly an ontological but an existential term. The *Atharva Veda* has a magician saying, "I do this truth" (*satyam kṛṇomi*), and the legends which tell of the "doing of truth" are common in the early literature. Gandhi carried on this tradition of 'truth-grasping' (*satyāgraha*) not only in public protest but also through experimentation in daily lite.

A concrete approach to truth appeared in Gandhi's definition and approach to God. He sought a concept of God which would be acceptable to all men, religious and non-religious alike. He formed a concept, moreover, which included both a definition of God's nature and the means for man to approach the divine. In his early life he worked with the notion of 'God is Truth,' but later reversed it to 'Truth is God.' He wrote in *Harijan* in 1935:

> God is Truth, but God is many other things also. That is why I say Truth is God. . . . Only remember that Truth is not one of the many qualities that we name. It is the living embodiment of God, it is the only Life, and I identify Truth with the fullest life, and that is how it becomes a concrete thing, for God is His whole creation, the whole Existence, and service of all that exists—Truth—is service to God.[7]

7. *Harijan*, May 25, 1935.

CHAPTER 2

For Whom the Bell Does Not Toll

> Ordinary people, soon forgotten . . . not for them any Martyr's Memorials or Eternal Flames.
>
> AMITAV GHOSH (*Shadow Lines*)

It is one of the biggest lies ever told that the Indians got their freedom too easily. Pointing out to the benefits like the English language, the rule of law, the railways and telegraph brought by the British rule, the Anglophiles attribute it to the essentially enlightened and benign nature of the British rule that gave in so easily to the non-violent agitation undertaken by the Congress under the leadership of Mahatma Gandhi. Citing the examples of Algeria and Indonesia, they hold that India did not have to pay the price of freedom in blood. That's why Indians, they say, take their freedom so lightly because they got it too easily. Consciously or unconsciously, they are vindicating the essentially civilizing mission of the British Empire in which the imperialists strongly believed till the end notwithstanding its essentially self-serving and highly exploitative nature. Apart from among the 'wogs' in large numbers which is perhaps understandable though not excusable, surprisingly a large number of Punjabis particularly those belonging to the older generation—among them B.K. Nehru of the ICS and a cousin of Pandit Nehru though he could easily belong to either or both the categories—subscribed to this ridiculous view even though it was the Punjabis on both sides of the border who suffered most heavily in 1947-8 during the course of Partition. B.K. Nehru was a Punjabi, albeit of Kashmiri descent, to boot. In his *Nice Guys Finish Second,* he wrote: 'I cannot help but contrast the comparative ease with which we got our freedom from the colonial power with the horrors which non-British European colonies had to suffer.' Like most of his Indian colleagues in the ICS he flourished greatly as a direct result of the exodus of their senior British colleagues with the transfer of power and he rose to the highest positions, not the least because of his close family connections to the first prime minister of India. Punjabis and many other Indians were not alone in thinking along these lines. Among foreigners, the popular author-duo Larry Collins and Dominique Lapierre similarly assert that India was fortunate unlike other colonial nations in not having to 'pay the price of their freedom with bloody wars'.[1]

Nothing could be farther from the truth. The theory of civilizing mission and overall beneficial nature of the British colonial regime has been blown sky high by Shashi Tharoor in his address to the Oxford Students Union the previous year (2015), which he has elaborated in his book during the course of which he demanded a formal apology and reparations, albeit on a token basis, from the British for the ex-tensive destruction wrought and systematic looting and plunder of India carried out during about 250 years of British stay in India.[2] New research recently published by Columbia University Press shows that in nearly two centuries from 1765 to 1938, Britain managed to drain as much as $45 trillion from India by imposing a highly exploitative tax and trade system. A mind boggling amount which is 17 times Britain's current GDP! Jason Hickel calls it 'a scam—theft on a grand scale'.[3] Even if one were to disregard at least 3 million who died during the Bengal Famine of 1943-4 on top of the countless millions who died in the earlier famines which used to strike one or the other part of India every four years or so with sickening regularity—a phenomenon which was unknown till the advent of the British in India and has not occurred since their departure, a point so convincingly brought out by Amartya Sen in his *Poverty and Famines*[4] the British rulers are still squarely to be blamed for at least 1 million killed and countless more injured, property worth nearly Rs. 20,000 million lost and about 10 to 12 million people displaced and reduced to absolute penury as a consequence of Partition-related disturbances in 1947 due to sheer callousness, ineptitude and mismanagement of the situation both politically and administratively by the British colonial regime in India as well as in London. As aptly observed by Andrew Roberts, it was the Punjab where most of the killings happened that paid the price of freedom in blood.[5] The ruthless crushing of the Mutiny in 1857, regarded by Indians as the first war of independence, was followed by the most brutal kind of bloody reprisals by the British rulers on the native populations to administer an unforgettable lesson. After peremptorily locking up the entire Congress leadership, the colonial regime proceeded to most brutally crush the Quit India movement launched by Mahatma Gandhi on 8 August 1942, which was the most popular mass movement to rock the British rule in India to its very foundations since the 1857 Mutiny. Keenly aware of the serious danger that this wildly popular agitation, which erupted spontaneously and quickly spread like wildfire to even small towns and remote villages all over India following the *en masse* arrest of Gandhi and the Congress leadership in a pre-emptive pre-dawn swoop on 9 August, represented a most serious threat since 1857 to their continuance in India at a time when the Japanese armies were virtually at the doorstep in the north-east and threatening to overrun India. The British pulled out all stops and struck back most viciously and brutally by unleashing its finely honed machinery of state terror, extensively employing the British army and air force to strike terror into the hearts of the people and to ruthlessly crush their resistance. A very large number of people who participated in this spontaneous uprising were thrown behind bars along with the Congress workers and subjected to inhuman tortures inside the prison. There were innumerable cases of police resorting to *lathi* charge, tear gassing and firing on agitators including students, women and children who took to streets in large numbers in response to Mahatma Gandhi's Quit India call. In industrial towns and cities like Jamshedpur, Dalmianagar, Howrah and Ahmedabad, workers stopped work in sympathy. Bombay Presidency, UP and Bihar in particular were the epicentres of this mass upheaval though other provinces like Bengal Presidency, Assam, Orissa, CP and Berar and Madras Presidency were also widely affected. It took almost a year of the most brutal kind of state repression involving also the machine-gunning of unarmed agitating civilians both from the ground and from the air before an uneasy kind of normalcy could be restored in eastern India. While the official figures put the numbers killed and wounded in police and military firing at 1,028 and 3,200 respectively, according to the unofficial figures the number killed was about 25,000. In *Discovery of India*, Pandit Nehru put the number killed in 1942 movement at about 10,000. Several villages were burnt down by officials on suspicion of involvement in the agitation to serve as a warning to others, and nine million rupees, a very large sum in those days, was levied as collective fine, which by its nature made no distinction between the actual participants and the non-participants in the offending act. By the end of the year, more than 100,000 persons were in jail without trial. Most of them were released only after the war came to an end in 1945.[6] Indeed, a very steep price had to be paid in blood, broken limbs and long imprisonment and huge monetary loss by the Indian people and their leaders at the hands of the British rulers and their minions for this mass uprising against colonial rule in 1942. Lord Linlithgow was the viceroy of India at that time and Lord Wavell was the C-in-C.

A similar brutal repression was unleashed by the colonial authorities against the Indian people during earlier mass agitations like the Non-Cooperation movements in 1921-2 and 1930-2 and salt law *satyagraha* undertaken by the Congress under the leadership of Gandhi against the British, but it is the repression in 1942 which in its intensity and the scale of death and destruction inflicted by the state that took the cake. However, a particularly notorious atrocity committed by the British during the earlier period which fully exposed the barbarous, cruel and bloodthirsty nature of the colonial regime was the pitiless shooting without adequate warning at an unarmed assembly, which had gathered to peacefully protest against the enactment of the infamous Rowlatt Act, at Jallianwala Bagh in Amritsar on 13 April 1919. It was Baisakhi, a major harvest festival in the Punjab, which falls every year on 13 April, when a large number of people from villages far and near flock to the Golden Temple, situated next to it, to pay obeisance after taking a dip in the holy *sarovar* (tank) surrounding it. As a matter of fact, at the time of the shooting, a large part of the assembly in Jallianwala

Bagh consisted of these devotees as it was a common meeting place or rendezvous point before proceeding to the temple and after returning from it, and being simple rural folk almost none of them had any political agenda. It was a combined force of Gurkhas and British troops under the direct command of a British officer, Brigadier-General Dyer, which undertook the firing that went on for long after the crowd had started dispersing under the first hail of bullets and stopped only because the troops had almost exhausted their stock of ammunition. There were very heavy casualties because Jallianwala Bagh is a garden enclosed completely from three sides by high walls and the only narrow entrance from the fourth side was blocked by the troops firing at them. The crowd therefore had nowhere to run or hide. To escape from the flying bullets coming at them thick and fast, many in utter desperation jumped into a well that was there and were drowned. This was followed by imposition of Martial Law in five districts of the Punjab including of course Amritsar during which the worst kind of atrocities and indignities were inflicted on civilian population at large to strike terror into the hearts of the people and to teach them a lesson for all times to come. While the official figures admitted to only about 400 people being killed and about 2,000 wounded, the Commission of Inquiry appointed by the Congress consisting of leading lawyers and barristers reported, after examining a large number of witnesses, that the number killed was about 2,000, which was not unlikely considering the number of rounds fired (1,650 according to official admission) in broad daylight by trained soldiers on unarmed civilians trapped in a small enclosed space without any cover and with no escape route. The authorities made no effort to remove the dead bodies and the strict enforcement of curfew prevented the relatives to collect the dead bodies of their kin. Even the injured were left suffering overnight without any medical aid.[7] Jallianwala Bagh incident which represented a turning point in India's quest for freedom from British rule lives in infamy for all times to come in the British colonial history in India. Very recently, *The Times*, London (11 September 2019) on its front page published a photograph of the Arch Bishop of Canterbury Most Reverend Justin Welby, the head of the Church of England and of the Anglican Church worldwide, prostrating himself full length in front of the Martyrs Memorial in Jallianwala Bagh and expressed his 'profound regret and shame' for the atrocity calling it a crime and a sin. Yet the British government has so far steadfastly refused to apologize ignoring strong calls from various quarters from time to time. The last prime minister Theresa May stopped just short of it when in her statement to Parliament in April 2019 just before the centenary of the massacre, she expressed regret. Another case of British bloody-mindedness.

The story of blood and gore shed in the course of India's struggle for independence would not be complete without making a passing reference to the INA, consisting mostly of men and officers of the Indian army who were taken prisoners of war by the Japanese during the Second World War, who later took up arms against the Allies alongside the Japanese under the charismatic leadership of Subhas Chandra Bose, and the mutiny of naval ratings in Bombay (now Mumbai) in February 1946 which quickly spread to several other naval establishments along the coast. Some air force and army establishments struck work in sympathy as also the mill workers and students in large numbers in Bombay, which was the epicentre. Although these events may not have had much military significance, the very fact that a significant numbers of the Indian members of the armed forces which formed the bedrock for the creation and conti-nuance of the British Empire in India had taken up arms against their colonial masters was not lost on the British. Apart from the numbers—it was not large, probably a few hundred only—who died in action fighting against the British in the north-east during the war, most of the remaining members of the INA running into several thousands were captured and subjected to unspeakable tortures in the name of interrogation by the military authorities and sought to be put on trial at the Red Fort in Delhi before military courts. That instantly converted them into national heroes in the eyes of their countrymen and leading Indian lawyers and barristers—among them was Pandit Nehru who donned the barrister's robe after a long layoff since joining active politics and the struggle for freedom—voluntarily came forward to defend them. There was a frenzied popular feeling all over the country especially in Calcutta against these trials. Between November 1945 when the first trial opened against a Muslim (Capt. Shahnawaz), a Hindu (Captain Prem Sehgal) and a Sikh (Captain Dhillon) officer and February 1946, there were huge public demonstrations in Calcutta in which police had to open fire killing forty demonstrators on the first occasion, thirty-five on the second occasion on 21 November, and eighty-four on the third occasion on 21 February 1946. The last two were jointly participated by the Congress, Muslim League and the Communists. 'Even the members of the Indian armed forces made no secret of their sympathy with the INA prisoners', leading Field Marshal Auchinleck to observe in his report that every Indian commissioned officer was a nationalist (Nitish Sengupta, *Bengal Divided*, pp. 107-8). Sensing the strong public sentiment throughout the country in favour of the INA prisoners and the strong likelihood that any precipitate action against them would cause a tremendous furore, the British authorities developed cold feet and made a major climb down regarding the trials.

The naval mutiny was brutally crushed by employing overwhelming military force. About 228 people, mostly civilians, were killed and 1,048 injured[8] despite clear indications to surrender from the hungry and thirsty sailors, whose supply of food and fresh water had been cut-off for many days. Before that, during the war in 1940, a Sikh squadron of a crack Tank regiment of the British Indian army had refused to embark for Africa at Bombay and had to be promptly disarmed and disbanded. Coming as it did from Sikh troops who had steadfastly stood loyal to the British ever since the last Anglo-Sikh War in 1849, including during the 1857 Mutiny, a few years later when the whole of north India had erupted against the British, sent shock waves across the British establishment. At the time of the naval mutiny in February 1946, severe disaffection was reported among the Indian rank and file in the Royal Indian Air Force and in the technical services of the army who happened to be better educated and hence more aware of and in broad sympathy with the freedom movement undertaken by the Congress, which was rocking the country from end to end. There were several reports of Indian personnel in *mufti* participating in the public meetings addressed by the nationalist leaders near cantonments. These developments no doubt caused alarm in the ruling circles, providing further indications that their time in India was up. Although there was no open insurrection except in the RIN which was the smallest service though the best educated, the situation was somewhat reminiscent of the period before the outbreak of the dreaded 1857 Mutiny.

In case the above was not enough, the blood bath and the extensive mayhem accompanying Partition leaves no room for doubt that both India and Pakistan paid a very heavy price indeed in blood and devastation for their freedom. It was literally a baptism by fire and gore. Human beings in millions were killed or injured or otherwise suffered terribly. Partition was a 'Greek tragedy' in the words of Nehru of humongous proportions for which history offers few parallels. Indeed few nations and people have paid more for their freedom. Arguing otherwise as many have tended to do would therefore be a travesty tantamounting to denial of history.

Although it is agreed all around that a great many people were killed as a result of Partition, but as to the actual numbers there has been a lot of debate and disagreement among the authors and scholars over the years and the number has varied from as low as 100,000 claimed by Mountbatten during his visit to London in November 1947 to as high as three million. The first off the block was Penderel Moon of the Punjab cadre of the ICS. He had been the deputy commissioner in key districts of Multan and Amritsar and thereafter Private Secretary to the Governor of Punjab before becoming a minister in the Muslim princely state of Bahawalpur lying along the border between India and Pakistan where he was serving at the time of Partition. Bahawalpur itself had experienced serious disturbances in the wake of Partition as recorded by him in his book *Divide and Quit.* He came up with a figure of 180,000 to 200,000 killed on both sides. He is best remembered for his phrase that during Partition 'the Hindus and Sikhs lost the most property and the Muslims lost the most lives'. Because of his long field experience, intimate local knowledge and his vast contacts among the officials at different levels as well as with the main political leaders in the Punjab across the board by virtue of the key positions held by him, the figures quoted by him commanded a certain could arise between an opponent and adversary. He individualized the protester's cause, ideals and methods. *Swarāj* (Indian Home Rule), which was India's cry for political independence was used by Gandhi and particularized to mean personal self-rule and self-control. A significant contribution of Gandhi to Indian ethic was to think and to act within the realm of the particular and the practical which was partially achieved through discipline. In political conflict Gandhi struggled to keep relationships flexible, open and in process. *Satyāgraha*, as a method of holding moral alternatives and achieving relative levels of truth and justice, is in its very nature flexible, creative and open to the future. Gandhi saw a life of non-violence as open to the contingencies of the creative process.

The key to Gandhi's social thought and concept of man is characterized in one word: *sarvodaya*. It literally means the uplift of all. The goal is to lift man both spiritually and socially to new levels of life and experience. Gandhi saw the rise of man and society as parallel and concomitant processes in history. He gave to India the means to enter history seriously and effectively. Gandhi's philosophy was a new emergent in the religious history of India because he brought *karma-yoga* not only into the historical process but made the *karma-yogin* an effective transformer of society. *Karma-yoga* for Gandhi was not just a means of self-realization, its primary and frequently sole goal in the past, but was a means to lift up both the individual and his society to greater realization. There is a ring of the prophet in Gandhi's teaching because he focused upon a decisive issue. He asked whether man could truly change. His effort was to make the *karma-yogin* the transformer of the socio-political world.

CHAPTER SEVEN

Educational Theory

> I have given many things to India. But this system of education together with its technique is, I feel, the best of them. I do not think I wll have anything better to offer the country.[1]

With these words Mahatma Gandhi launched the Wardha Scheme in 1937, a national programme in basic education (*Nai Talim*), which culminated many years of experimentation in education. His educational thought evolved out of his experiences in education within his family and four *āśrams* before it was formulated and announced to the country. It was precipitated, however, by Gandhi's effort to raise up non-violent men and a non-violent society. Much like his training of the

1. M. K. Gandhi, *The Problem of Education* (Ahmedabad: Navajivan Publishing House, 1962) p.v. Gandhi wrote extensively on education and the compilations of his writings are: *Educational Reconstruction* (Wardha: Hindustani Talimi Sangh, 1939); *Towards New Education*, edit. Bharatan Kumarappa (Ahmedabad : Navajivan Publishing House, 1953) ; *The Task before Indian Students*, comp. R. K. Prabhu (Ahmedabad: Navajivan Publishing House, 1961); *Gandhi's Thoughts on Education*, comp T. S. Avinashilingam (New Delhi: Ministry of Education, 1958); *To the Students* (Ahmedabad: Navajivan Publishing House, 1949) ; *True Education* (Ahmedabad: Navajivan Publishing House, 1962) ; *My Views on Education*, edit. Anand T. Hingorani (Bombay: Bharatiya Vidya Bhavan, 1970) ; *Basic Education* (Ahmedabad: Navajivan Press, 1951) ; *Message to Students*, edit, A. T. Hingorani (Allahabad: Leader Press, 1958).

non-violent individual, his effort in education advanced from family to followers in the *āśrams* and, finally, to all India.

What urged him to place his theory on a national scale was an abhorrence of the British system of education imposed upon India. Considering the British system as impractical and destructive of the Indian imagination, Gandhi called it an "unmitigated evil."[2] He thought it ignored everything India had discovered in its educational experience, such as children integrated with environment, strong pupil-teacher relationships, identity with a people and an appreciation of Indian culture. The most devastating effect was the creation of a new caste, an English-speaking class. Hence Gandhi's plan for the nation was an attempt to restore the national and social continuum disrupted by European imposition. British education placed literacy within the context of a literary education as its principal goal. Gandhi sharply distinguished literacy from knowledge and wrote in *Harijan* in 1937, that "Literacy in itself is no education."[3] Since the school was an extension of the home for Gandhi, he sought continuity in language and culture between the school and home. He spoke, moreover, against an emphasis on literature as a basic context for learning. He called for a broader basis in education and not just training in literature and literacy. He believed that the building of character, the development of skills in living and working, and the imparting of an appreciation and understanding of Indian culture were far more crucial. In his *Message to Students* Gandhi posed a question which indicated the genesis of his concerns: ". . . are you receiving an education. . .which will draw the best out of you?"[4]

The purpose of Gandhian education is to raise man to a higher moral and spiritual order through the full development of the individual and the evolution of a new man, a *satyāgrahi*, a non-violent personality. Everything in Gandhi's thought is related to the universal value of truth and *ahiṃsā* and directed toward the realization of God and a new humanity. Thus his educational scheme is best understood and appreciated within

2. *Message to Students*, p. 14.
3. *Harijan*, July 31, 1937.
4. *Message to Students*, p. 5.

the framework of the rest of his philosophy. Truth and *ahiṃsā* are the two principles entering into every aspect of his thought and activity. There is an identity of ideals between truth and *ahiṃsā* and the Wardha Scheme for basic education. Truth, non-violence, service to humanity and fearlessness were Gandhi's goals, and education became the means to these goals. "The whole scheme of education is based on truth and non-violence," wrote the Mahatma.[5] He believed education was the natural context for the cultivation of non-violent values since *ahiṃsā* could be discovered and exercised in the relations among children. The cultivation of non-violence in the individual and collectively within the academic community was the goal pursued in every human activity in the schools The non-violent personality, the *satyāgrahi,* was the principal and immediate focus of education for Gandhi. Truth can neither be attained nor lived without non-violence and, consequently, the school must impart non-violent values.

The creation of a new personality consists in the building of character which became for Gandhi the end of all knowledge. Character building was the fundamental enterprise in the school he envisioned. He looked upon the development of personality as far more significant than the accumulation of intellectual tools and academic knowledge. He sought the mastery of the

5. M. K. Gandhi, quoted in Viswanath Sahai Mathur, edit. *Gandhiji as an Educationist, A Symposium* (Delhi: Metropolitan Book Co., Ltd., 1951), p. 82. Many secondary works on Gandhi on education exist; a through study is M. S. Patel, *The Educational Philosophy of Mahatma Gandhi* (Ahmedabad: Navajivan Press, 1953). Also comprehensive is N. P. Pillai, *The Educational Aims of Mahatma Gandhi* (Trivandrum: Kalyanmandir Publications, 1959). Other helpful studies are J. B. Kripalani, *The Latest Fad, Basic Education* (Sevagram, Wardha: Hindustani Talimi Sangh, 1948); K. L. Shrimali, *The Wardha Scheme, The Gandhian Plan of Education for Rural India* (Udaipur: Vidya Bhavan Society, 1949) ; Shriman Narayan, *Towards Better Education* (Ahmedabad: Navajivan Publishing House, 1969); Marni Tata Ramji, *The Concept of Personality in the Educational Thought of Mahatma Gandhi* (New Delhi: National Council of Educational Research & Training, 1969); I. B. Verma, *Basic Education: A Reinterpretation* (Agra: Sri Ram Mehra & Co., 1969); G. Ramanathan, *Education from Dewey to Gandhi, The Theory of Basic Education* (Bombay: Asia Publishing House, 1962).

whole personality, and since truth is the basis of personality education should develop the highest truth possible in the mind, the spirit and the body. Good education is "that which draws out and stimulates the spiritual, intellectual and physical faculties of children."[6] Gandhi's concept of personality was based on the ideal man of the *Bhagvad Gītā*, as was his notion of the *satyāgrahi*, one standing firmly rooted in wisdom and truth (*sthitaprajñā*), one fully developed. The qualities of the harmonious personality, likewise, are of the same cast as those of the paradigm of the *Gītā* and the non-violent personality, such as self-control, universally non-violent, selfless social activity, fearlessness, with all life centered in truth. Schools and colleges thus become the context for character formation.[7]

The building of character in terms of non-violence and truth is a form of spiritual education. But Gandhi's goal was the spiritual refashioning of the whole personality through education.

Gandhian education has been characterized as encompassing the head, the heart and the hands.

> Man is neither mere intellect, nor the gross animal body, nor the heart or soul alone. A proper and harmonious combination of all the three is required for the making of the whole man and constitutes the true economics of education.[8]

The cultivation of the heart—emotions and feelings—consists in the refinement of human emotions and impulses; it promotes feelings of love, sympathy and fellowship. The keynote of Gandhi's thought is creative activity in education. He wanted education to deal more with the concrete, and so made manual work and crafts an integral part of the school system. He believed that a child up to fourteen or fifteen has a natural capacity to grasp the concrete.

6. *Harijan*, September 1, 1937.
7. *To the Students*, p. 107. It should be noted that Gandhi's interpretation of the *Gītā* is somewhat unique, for he views it as supporting non-violence even though Kṛṣṇa in the *Gītā* instructs Arjuna to kill. Gandhi would interpret it allegorically as an interior and spiritual battle within man himself.
8 Mathur, *Gandhiji as an Educationist*, p. 34.

Mind and heart can only be refined if the hand is brought into activity, drawing the educative process more into life. He thought that students could be self-supporting to some degree and this could be accomplished if the child worked manually as he learned. Gandhi's notion of self-supporting education cannot be separated from the non-violent personality, for the *satyāgrahi* must be self-supporting at every stage of his growth. He placed emphasis on the child's experiences in daily life and work, experiences which foster cooperative activity and not competitive individualism. An educational programme, moreover, must be attractive enough for the student to enthusiastically approve it himself. If education is true to life, it requires continual testing. Gandhi handed over the Wardha Scheme to Zakir Hussain for experimentation, because he believed that education required the "boldest experiments."[9] All Gandhi's socio-political principles entered his plan for national education, but experimentation was the one essential for education to be true to life. He placed education into the larger context of his thought and practice, that is, the development of the person materially, morally and spiritually. Such development, he believed, brought about the non-violent personality who would serve his fellow man.

Gandhi's educational theory had a clear social orientation. His educational principles are evident in *Hind Swarāj*, the 1909 social manifesto, in which he enumerated an eighteen point programme for social and political reconstruction. He aimed at the time to reconstruct Indian society which implied a reconstruction of education. The school is basically a community linked to social achievements. He envisioned true education coming about primarily through a particular pattern of life in a community and not merely through instruction. The realization of the spiritual society was a prelude to the realization of truth and God. Hence education had a social setting and purpose whereby human perfection could be achieved in a community and in the creation of the perfect society. The school must be in Gandhi's plan an organized society itself which is engaged in some fruitful activtiy contributing to the greater society. A social orientation in education, he believed, strengthens

9. *Young India*, Sept. 30, 1926.

social and cooperative attitudes in a practical manner. Yet the school has the special task of preparing citizens of the new society, in this case the non-violent society, by teaching youth to live together as a community on the basis of cooperation, truth and *ahiṃsā*. The social orientation Gandhi gave to the schools was similar to what he tried to achieve in his *āśrams*. He conceived the Sevagram Āśram as a place where the community was created, where equality ruled, where hatred was stamped out and honesty was required. The most visible aspects of Sevagram were cooperation, sympathy and self-help. Gandhi anticipated the school as the builder of the new non-violent society because his fundamental conception of society was spiritual: "The whole human society is a ceaseless growth, an unfoldment in terms of spirituality."[10]

A programme in basic education, Gandhi maintained, must assuage the poverty of India. He urged students to organize social service in cities and villages in order to help the poor and weaker members of society. Education was a special tool in the reform of Indian village life. With eighty per cent of Indians living in villages, Gandhi realized that education could spearhead a silent but forceful social revolution. One major reason he advocated education through the teaching of craft was to check the decay of the villages. Education through a craft, he believed, would place the destiny of the masses in their own hands and give them a sense of dignity and identity. It would eradicate any dependency on foreign imports and establish relationships between the city and the village. Written into the Wardha Scheme of education were means to revive village industries, crafts and the spirit of village life. The Gandhian plan must be evaluated within the context of village education or it will be misunderstood and misjudged. Nonetheless, he saw the basic plan as developing a national consciousness. He strongly spoke for education that would meet all the needs of the people, social, economic, political and cultural.

Gandhi believed that especially in education "We are the makers of our destiny."[11] If education is the builder of the new non-violent society, schools must be self-sufficient and

10. Mathur, *Gandhiji as an Educationist*, p. 87.

11 *Harijan*, June 8, 1947.

self-supporting. This is the heart of Gandhi's emphasis on the social orientation in education. He is not introducing something novel but has in mind classical monasticism which has always been self-supporting and self-sufficient. Education through a craft could possibly render education self-supporting. It would certainly render the individual self-supporting in the future. Gandhi wrote: "Self-sufficiency is not an *a priori* condition, but to me, it is the acid test."[12] Maintaining that three generations of non-violent life within a society are necessary to change a people, Gandhi looked to education to give people the self-support necessary for a non-violent society to actualize and stabilize itself. Hence the genesis of the new social order would be the schools.

M.S. Patel has called Gandhi's educational philosophy naturalistic in setting, idealistic in aims and pragmatic in method.[13] Naturalism in education is apparent from Gandhi's tendency toward simplicity in life, in language and literature and in his opposition to pedantry. Basic education was natural for he saw it as an extension of the home as related to the child's environment. He believed in the essential goodness of children, and that education must follow the natural and progressive growth of both the child and the child's culture. Learning within the Gandhian school takes place in an atmosphere of play which is child-centered and respects the freedom of the child. The emphasis on activity, a craft common to the locality, contributed to a naturalistic setting.

On the other hand, a definite idealism for which he was severely criticized is also found in Gandhi's educational theory. His basic aim to develop a spiritual man within a spiritual society has been historically the idealist goal in educational theory. Conceiving education as a preparation for total life and not necessarily for a specific profession is another idealist goal. Yet his ideal of self-realization, that is, the more perfect attainment of truth and non-violence, were the most motivating educational goals for him.

12. Mathur, *Gandhi as an Educationist*, p. 51.

13. See M. S. Patel, *The Educational Philosophy of Mahatma Gandhi*, p. 179 ; also see I. B. Verma, *Basic Education: A Reinterpretation*, for the following discussion.

In its methodology his system leaves much for the ingenuity and creativeness of the child since the child is called to growth through self-activity. As a saint-politician, Gandhi was a pragmatical individual and pragmatism was explicit in his view of education. For example, the development of manual skills is integral to the Wardha Scheme which was focused around three interrelated centres: physical environment, social environment and a craft. The Wardha plan envisaged primary education, compulsory and universal, for seven years covering all subjects except English, plus a vocational skill. Primary education was to take the place of the classical primary, middle and high school plan initiated by the British. Progress in the schools was to be pragmatic, based on rigorous habits of investigation and experimentation through scientific thinking. In advancing the principle of self-sufficiency, Gandhi insisted that the schools be self-supporting to the degree that the teachers were paid for their services. Condemning bookishness and excessive verbalizing in teaching, he advanced realistic education in his effort to move the schools into the affairs of society. He wanted to close the gap between education and life by drawing upon the cultural, social and vocational potentialities of students.

Gandhi is consonant with John Dewey who also believed that elements of social life should be integrated in the school system. Their ideas arose from the divorce of school and home. Dewey, also advocating an adult occupation in the schools, said that Gandhi was "One step ahead of all the other systems and is full of immense potentialities."[14] Gandhi met Madame Maria Montessori first in India in 1915 and again in Rome in 1931. She recognized that Gandhi's educational principles which she saw exemplified in his own life were basic to her system. In the course of years Gandhi evolved not only a pragmatic but a clearly defined work ethic in politics, religion and education. It has been described as an evangelical work ethic because it was a religious doctrine of full participation in the secular order.[15] His work ethic emerged from a

14. Narayan, *Towards Better Education*, p. 139.
15. See Joseph W. Elder, "The Gandhian Ethic of Work in India," in *Religious Ferment in Asia*, edit. Robert J. Miller (Wichita: The University Press of Kansas, 1974), pp. 51ff.

complex of Indian and non-Indian sources as his autobiography testified from experiences in South Africa and England. His views, however, developed independently of non-Indian writers and were really a response to his own experience and his interpretation of the Hindu scriptures. The parallel thought that Gandhi discovered in other systems and writers merely confirmed him to proceed with more determination than previously. His work ethic as it is found in education is one such example. The similarities between Gandhian education and the work of Dewey and Montessori are of interest not because of mutual influences one upon the other but because Gandhi received confirmation in the course he had set for himself.

It has been observed that Gandhi restored the hand to its legitimate place in education. Although not directly influenced by educationists such as Pestalozzi, Herbart, and Froebel, he shared their insight in the need to assimilate knowledge through work. The use of a craft at all levels and in all stages of education was Gandhi's specification of education as a *karma-yoga*. Early in his career he had developed the notion of 'Bread Labour,' and this ethic was operative in his activities in South Africa in 1904.[16] Upon reading John Ruskin's *Unto this Last*, he was reinforced in the belief that a life of labour is a life worth living. He put into practice the work ethic first at the Phoenix Farm in Transvaal, and by 1910, in the Tolstoy Farm, 'Bread Labour' had become integral to its operation and had become a refined concept. "To live man must work," Gandhi maintained.[17] He meant some specific bodily activity, accepted voluntarily, with social service as its goal. He was again reinforced in his work ethic upon reading the Russian writers, Leo Tolstoy and T.M. Bondaref, and also upon his own interpretation of the *Gītā* and the *Īśopaniṣad.* The introduction of craft in education was then an extension of his theory of 'Bread Labour' and the specification of *karma-yoga* which raised education to the level of service, a religious service. He observed that:

16. *Ibid.*

17. M. K. Gandhi, *From Yervada Mandir*, trans. Valji G. Desai (Ahmedabad: Navajivan Press, 3rd ed. 1945), p. 35.

> He who spins before the poor inviting them to do likewise serves God as no one else does. . . . Spinning, therefore, for such is the greatest prayer, the greatest worship, the greatest sacrifice.[18]

The introduction of craft in education, Gandhi believed, is intended to teach through concrete life situations in order that what is taught can be assimilated into life. The craft becomes the sources out of which experiences and activities are born. He envisioned the education of the whole man through craft and the whole of education developed through the craft. Craft in the schools was not to be a mechanical thing but to be used scientifically wherein the child knows why the craft is introduced and how it is assimilated in the educative process. Gandhi proposed with the utilization of craft a change in the medium of instruction which ultimately altered the character of and language through which education was usually imparted. His conception of craft is not a mere addition of a subject to the curriculum but is a radical change in educational methodology. Labour in Gandhian education is the unifying and integrating factor because its goal is to combine the intellectual, the scientific and the physical growth of students. Gandhi considered productive manual activity as the perfect medium of education especially between the ages of seven and fourteen.[19]

Probably the major factor in Gandhi's educational reform was that all intellectual instruction be imparted through the instrumentality of the craft.[20] This implied that manual labour, intelligently correlated with an academic subject, was the best means for intellectual growth. Children must be taught the dignity of labour and learn to regard it as the means of intellectual growth. Gandhi believed that the child would take easily to work because it entertained and stimulated the intellect. "The core of my suggestion is that handicrafts are to be taught not merely for productive work, but for developing the intellects of pupils."[21] It was important that the craft selected be rich in

18. *Young India*, Sept. 24, 1925.
19. Hussain, *Education in the World of Tomorrow* (Bombay: The Progressive Group, 1945), p. 15.
20. Kripalani, *The Latest Fad, Basic Education,* pp. 66-67.
21. *Harijan*, Sept. 11, 1937.

educational opportunities and easily correlated with daily life. Also pertinent were the local conditions which should favourably support the craft selected. In the plan of basic education designed for the first seven years of school, Gandhi recommended the craft predominant in the locality, for example, spinning, carpentry, gardening and agriculture. After basic education, that is, beyond the fourteenth year, the craft should become more sophisticated, such as mechanics, electricity, medicine, commerce, printing and the domestic arts. Each school should have five or six crafts in order to give a variety of opportunities to the student. Craft-centered education is not necessarily production; it does not have as its goal the training of craftsmen but the utilization of craft activity for educative purposes. Craft is the genesis of educative experience for Gandhi. Yet craft is both a means and an end. The product of the craft must be economically usable. In the Wardha Scheme all education around a craft and the product of the craft was to be economically remunerative in order to defray the costs of education, at least the salaries of the teachers. The connection between craft as a medium of education and education as economically self-sufficient was important to Gandhi. Unless the latter is true, the first fails. He maintained that only remunerative craft work would be done with care and be a scientific improvement in the educative process. In practice he found that productivity was an essential condition for any craft to succeed as an element of correlated instruction.

Gandhi considered the introduction of craft his unique contribution to education for he believed that it would refashion education, society in general and the personality of youth. In the West correlation in education is accomplished through the interpenetration of many subjects, but in the Gandhian plan it is achieved through the interpenetration of manual labour in many subjects. Since craft is both a means and an end, it is "the convening point for instruction in all other subjects."[22] Craft and subject must be correlated to the physical and social environment since the principle of self-activity operative in correlation bears intimate relationship to the needs of the student and his familiar social world. The correlation of craft and

22. Mathur, *Gandhiji as an Educationist*, p. 82.

subject, according to Gandhi, was the principal means of relating the child to the villages, and ultimately, the villages to the cities. The technique of correlation assures that the craft becomes a medium of education and not of mere vocational training. If the craft is to relate the child to life, it must find the natural point of correlation with human activities and interests and extend to the whole curriculum. Correlation is the technique to bind education to the child's life and beyond. In short, it is an attempt to combine hand-culture and mind-culture.

Gandhi never worked out the details and technique of correlation. He knew that the technique had not been evolved, and that he had given it only an ideological basis. Yet what did emerge in his *āśram* experiments with correlation was the necessity for resourceful and cooperative teachers having an experimental attitude, who would exchange their experiences and keep scientific records of their successes and failures. The capacity for successful correlation depended upon the unity of the craft itself as an integrative element and upon its comprehensiveness whereby it could naturally be extended to other areas of knowledge. Three stages eventually were developed in correlation: first, the recollection of an element of knowledge already assimilated from the craft; secondly, the forming of a relationship from that element of knowledge to an academic subject; thirdly, the drawing out of a new element of knowledge bound to the previous one by the newly established relationship. Since correlative teaching aimed at establishing a medium of instruction encompassing the total mass of knowledge, over-strained or spurious correlation had to be avoided. Faulty correlation is harmful because it advances poor thinking and no real transmission of knowledge. Correlation, consequently, must not be forced. It is neither unilateral, that is, one subject correlated with one activity, nor bilateral, that is, knowledge and activity correlated simultaneously but is multilateral, correlation of many subjects with a craft-activity. The entire academic context is correlated with the craft.

Basic education through correlation was directed toward the integration of the student and the integration of curriculum. The Gandhian curriculum consisted of the craft, the mother tongue of the student, mathematics, social studies, natural science, music and drawing, and Hindustani. There was no instruction in either religion or English. Gandhi considered Hindustani the most opportune common language because it would be familiar to both the Hindu and Muslim communities. Hindustani is the same spoken language as Hindi and Urdu which differ only in script. Primary education, according to Gandhi, should employ as few books as possible and most teaching should be oral. Hence he suggested that the first year at school be completely without books. The time-table in basic education was carefully worked out by Gandhi himself: craft, three hours and twenty minutes a day; music, drawing and mathematics, forty minutes; social studies and natural science, thirty minutes; and physical training, ten minutes. The scheduling indicated the centrality he gave to craft-centered education.

Gandhi offered his plan to the whole nation. He not only saw it viable as national education for the young but also for higher education as well. Since his basic conception was to organically relate education to Indian social, economic and political life, he thought it should be relevant for higher education also. "I would revolutionize college education and relate it to national necessity," he announced.[23] He wanted to reorientate university life and relate it fully to Indian life. In fact he saw university education as a natural extension of his basic education plan. Many of the arts in the colleges, he believed, were both a waste of time and a cause of unemployment. University education should be a continuation of basic education, and it should be coordinated and brought into line with primary education. Although diversified institutions should exist, he saw the key principles of his educational theory relevant in all situations. Government should not administer higher education, according to the Mahatma, and colleges and universities should be left to private enterprise. In this way the national needs in industry, technology, the arts and letters can be better met. Hence in Gandhi's view basic education is not necessarily a preparation for new forms of learning at the advanced level but is the foundation out of which higher education naturally and organically develops.

Indira Miri believes that the most effective point in

23. *Educational Reconstruction*, p. 5.

Gandhi's plan consists in the pattern of living for teacher and student alike and not in his syllabus or curriculum.[24] The teacher of the Gandhian hue has been described as a lamp-post, a sign-board, a dissolvent, a processor, one who saves the pupil from a tyranny of words. The ideal teacher is one who consistently follows truth and *ahiṃsā*, one who is a practitioner of non-violence. Good education, according to Gandhi, takes place in association with a teacher who is non-violent. He believed that a teacher who doesn't inculcate truth leads students to perdition.[25] Speaking of the sacred work of the teacher, he wrote:

> Every one of us has good inherent in the soul, it needs to be drawn out by the teachers, and only those teachers can perform this sacred function whose own character is unsullied, who are always ready to learn and to grow from perfection to perfection.[26]

The teacher is particularly relevant for the education of the heart for "education of heart could only be done through the living touch of the teacher."[27] He called upon teachers to cultivate their own effective life and to encounter their student with a "heart-contact."[28] Gandhi advocates devotion to the teacher (*guru-bhakti*). In terms of the classical teacher-disciple relationship, the *guru* in Gandhi's estimation should be the epitome of devotion in order to elicit devotion from the student. He felt that in the absence of devotion to the teacher education would be dissipated and the building of character difficult to achieve. Gandhi, of course, anticipated a non-violent personality in the teacher, but the prevalent trait of a teacher was devotion to students, devotion to service and to God. The teacher has a mother's role in primary education wherby he is fully present to the student, nurtures him, lives with him and brings him to levels of greater

24. Indira Miri, *Mahatma Gandhi's Educational Theory* (New Delhi: Gandhian Thought, n.d.), p. 5.
25. *Young India*, Feb. 21, 1929.
26. *Young India*, Nomber 7, 1936.
27. *Young India*, September 1, 1921.
28. *Young India*, April 4, 1929.

maturity. "One who cannot take the place of a mother cannot be a teacher," wrote Gandhi in *My Views on Education*. Discussing the ideal teacher, he said:

> I have not used the word teacher in this article: I throughout used the word 'mother-teacher' in its place. Because the teacher must really be a mother to the children . . . . The child should never feel that he is being taught. Let her simply keep her eye upon him and guide him.[29]

While addressing five thousand teacher-applicants for his schools in basic education in 1938, he urged them not only to cultivate non-violent virtues but also to express non-violence daily in contact with their pupils. A teacher who was not a non-violent person and who could not communicate non-violence to students would fail, according to Gandhi, along with the school. Athough teaching without development of the spirit was of little use to him, spiritual development was always more difficult than physical and intellectual training: "And the exercise of the spirit entirely depends on the life and character of the teacher."[30] By spiritual development and the exercise of the spirit Gandhi meant, in particular, education of the heart.

The Wardha Scheme left out religion as a separate academic subject, because "religions as they are taught and practised today lead to conflict rather than unity."[31] On the other hand, Gandhi thought that truths common to all religions could and should be taught to all children. The Wardha syllabus used scriptural texts from world religions, and religious history was integral to social studies. Nonetheless, Gandhi excluded the teaching of religion *ex professo* because he saw religion in India as historically divisive and weakening. He believed that the state should provide facilities wherein every community gave religious training but not at the cost of the state. Religious education should be the sole concern of religious communities. At the same time, Gandhi's educational plan stood within the

29. *True Education*, p. 147.
30. Avinashilingam, *Gandhiji's Thoughts on Education*, p. 8.
31. Pillai, *The Educational Aims of Mahatma Gandhi*, p. 195.

general context of morality and the religion which he himself professed.

He advocated the teaching of classical principles of ethics which are found in all religions. "These should certainly be taught to the children and that should be regarded as adequate religious instruction so far as the schools under the Wardha Scheme are concerned."[32] He considered the teaching of a universal code of ethics as the function of the state. He fostered neither denominationalism nor anything which could prompt factionalism between Hindu and Muslim in the schools. Nonetheless, for a liberal education, he belived, a reverent study of other religions was necessary. If this were initiated, he cautioned that it be done in a spirit of broad-mindedness, reverence and tolerance. If adequately done the study of other religions would give the student a reassurance in his own tradition and a better appreciation for it. Gandhi tried to create an equal respect for all religions. Religion, for him, stood on the same footing as culture and civilization, where preservation means the assimilation of the best.

Gandhi's notion of religious education is the cultivation of universal love and brotherhood; it is "instruction in the universal essentials of religion."[33] In practice religious education is formation in fundamental virtues such as truth and *ahimsā*. Long before he publicly entered into education, he wrote in *Young India*:

> To me religion means truth and *ahimsa* or rather truth alone, because truth include *ahimsa*, *ahimsa* being the necessary and indispensable means for its discovery. Therefore anything that promotes the practice of these virtues is a means for imparting religious education and the best way to do this, in my opinion, is for the teachers rigorously to practise these virtues in their own person.[34]

Gandhi did not distinguish between religion and morality, since the development of one meant for him the inclusion of

32. Shrimali, *The Wardha Scheme*, pp. 224-25
33. Mathur, *Gandhiji as an Educationist*, p. 64ff.
34. *Young India*, December 6, 1928.

the other. He detected, however, obstacles in teaching about religion. He viewed Hinduism being so subtle that he could not easily suggest how to teach it. Recommending that the *Gītā*, *Rāmāyaṇa* and *Mahābhārata* be taught as a means of introducing students to their rich spiritual and culural heritage, he would go no further to specify instruction in Hinduism. "In this respect," he said, "the choice of the teacher is more important than laying down the course of instruction."[35] The important thing was to manifest tolerance and non-violence to students.

35. *Atmoddhar*, Vol. II, p. 135, cited in *True Education*, p. 158.

CHAPTER EIGHT

Praxis and Significance

Gandhi's experimentation was fully conducted within his *āśrams*. His educational ideals emerged from a lifetime of training that he supervised within the Phoenix Settlement, the Tolstoy Farm, the Sabarmati Āśram and the Satyāgraha Āśram. Although he began to teach his wife, Kasturbai, and his four sons individually, as soon as he settled in South Africa his basic educational ideals started taking shape with the founding of the Phoenix Settlement in 1904. Here he began serious ascetical training and experimentation in fasting, celibacy and dietetics. Three of Gandhi's four sons did not attend public schools but received their education solely from him, and the fourth, the oldest, when he broke away from his father went to a high school in Ahmedabad. In a letter to his son Manilal, written from the Volksrust prison in 1909, he confirmed the notion that education is the development of character and a virtuous life:

> Now I have read a great deal in the prison. . .All confirm the view that education does not mean a knowledge of letters but it means character building. It means a knowledge of duty. . .If this is the true view, and it is to my mind the only true view, you are receiving the best education possible. What can be better than that you should have the opportunity of nursing mother and cheerfully bearing her ill temper, or than looking after Chanchi and

> anticipating her wants and behaving to her so as not to make her feel the absence of Harilal . . . If you succeed in doing this well, you have received more than half your education . . . As soon as a boy reaches the age of discretion, he is taught to realize his responsibilities. Every boy from such age onward should practice continence in thought and deed, truth likewise and the not-taking of any life. . .If you practice these three virtues, if they become part of your life, so far as I am concerned you will have completed your education—your training. Armed with them, believe me you will earn your bread in any part of the world and you will have paved the way to acquire a true knowledge of the soul, yourself and God.[1]

In 1910 with the help of Herman Kallenbach, a German, Gandhi founded the Tolstoy Farm, a rural community for political resisters and their families outside of Johannesburg, South Africa. Classes were formed with Gandhi, Kallenbach and Pragji Desai as the principal teachers. Gandhi first met Kallenbach in South Africa and the two collaborated closely in dietary experiments; Gandhi, moreover, trained himself in fasting with the help of Kallenbach. Kallenbach was an important aid to Gandhi in integrating manual work and education. Kallenbach went to a Trappist monastery to observe the integration of work and prayer in the lives of the monks, and he learned the craft of sandal making during his stay with the monks. The Tolstoy Farm became an autonomous and self-sustaining community with every activity and service necessary for life done on its own premises. The population of the farm when it was not filled with resisters consisted of twenty to thirty children and forty or fifty adults. Imposing strict vegetarian rules and prohibiting smoking and drinking, Gandhi began to train his followers in the ascetical disciplines as a preparation for non-violence. The perception emerged at this time that education should be imparted by parents with the minimum of outside help. Since character formation was the special task of parents, Gandhi did not consider himself primarily as a teacher. Talking of this period in his autobiography, he

1. Fischer, *The Life of Mahatma Gandhi*, pp. 91-92.

recalled that he saw himself as the father of the Tolstoy Farm, where the children were Hindus, Muslims, Parsis and Christians, and in this role he took upon himself the task of education. The two principal tenets of Gandhi's future educational theory were clear to him at this time: education consisted in character building and imparting a useful manual vocation.[2]

When Gandhi and his *āśram* colony returned to India at the end of the South African conflict, C. F. Andrews, Tagore's close associate in education, took *satyāgrahis* to Santiniketan in Bengal. Arriving at the Tagore school, Gandhi persuaded the entire community of a hundred or more children and teachers to enter into the activity of the kitchen, cooking and cleaning, and the entire scope of *āśram* work. Gandhi was much impressed by Tagore's advances in education but believed Santiniketan neither austere nor simple enough. When Gandhi and his group left Santiniketan to establish their own *āśram*, the austerities he had introduced there with Tagore's acquiescense, gradually disappeared. Even in modern times the Tagore school recalls this period in celebrating a Gandhi Day.

Gandhi desired his own *āśram* to be in his home province of Gujarat. In May 1915, he began his first Indian *āśram* at Kochrab and then shortly after across the Sabarmati river from Ahmedabad. The Sabarmati Āśram was Gandhi's home for the next twenty years, and from this rural hermitage he led the Congress Party and the freedom movement. From the very beginning of his Indian experience, Gandhi saw national education as an activity of the *āśram*. All the principles which he publicly advocated in the formal Wardha Scheme were first experimented with at the Sabarmati Āśram and received their first articulation in early years of the *āśram*, namely, character formation, teachers as examples of truth and *ahiṃsā*, education conducive to the welfare of the villages, and the inclusion of manual training with intellectual growth. He looked upon Sabarmati as a Gujarat Vidyapith, that is, a university training in non-violence, which in 1920 took as its motto the Indian adage, "Education is that which liberates." In 1921 the Gujarat Vidyapith was established as a national university at

2. *Autobiography*, pp. 333-35.

the height of the non-cooperation movement to train people of character and ability to conduct *swarāj* in the villages. It was at this time that Gandhi identified education with *swarāj*: "We shall be fit for *swarāj* to the extent that we are successful among our students. Work with students is the only instrument with which to fashion *swarāj*"[3] It must be recalled that Gandhi during these years modified the meaning of *swarāj*, which in the national independence movement meant "Home-Rule" but in Gandhi's reconceptualization meant "self-rule". Only once in the early 1920s did Gandhi call for non-cooperation among students enrolled in the British schools. He called off the strike shortly afterwards and by 1924 had begun to support the national schools. In a speech in 1920 he said that as long as India was not prepared to sacrifice the type of education it was then receiving, it would be impossible to achieve freedom for the country.[4] His objective in education was to give villagers autonomy and identity, a sense that their destiny was in their own hands. The Gujarat Vidyapith was declared illegal in the early 1930's because its members had participated in the non-violent campaigns of 1931-32.

The last *āśram* Gandhi established was at Sevagram, near Wardha, in central India. It was founded in 1932 and became the home for the Mahatma during his remaining years. All the principles that he had developed in both *āśram* life and education were put into immediate operation at Sevagram. The Satyāgraha Āśram at Sevagram soon became the model of non-violent life for all India. It was from this Āśram that Gandhi advanced his national plan for basic education. It became the centre in which national conferences were held on education. The Satyāgraha Āśram was the fullest expression of Gandhi's vision and praxis in education, and he saw it as the place where his ideals could be lived in a real and pragmatic way. Since he had a personal need for the community life of the *āśram*, he realized early in his career the necessity to create a community where people were non-violent. The Gandhian *āśram* was "a community of men of religion," where gradually evolved the concept of a spiritual community within

3. *To the Students*, p. 54.
4. *The Problem of Education*, p. 14.

āśram life.[5] He had founded the Phoenix Settlement in Natal, South Africa, for the express purpose of establishing economic equality within a community. Phoenix became a religious institution only after he had taken the vow of *brahmācārya* (celibacy) and the *āśram* became a training ground for *satyāgraha.* But it was Gandhi's focus upon education which most formed the *āśram* into a community, because Gandhian education carried the religion of service into daily life and activity.

After forty years of preparation Gandhi announced in *Harijan* the call to the entire country to revolutionize education according to his plan. It came as a shock and critics reacted strongly, calling it reactionary, anti-revolutionary, medieval, fadist, impractical and excessively spiritual.[6] The plan contained all he had previously worked out, but he specified handicraft by identifying spinning as the most suitable craft for rural India. A conference was called at Wardha in October 1937, to examine Gandhi's plan, a conference which he chaired as president. The report of this conference gave birth to what is known as the Wardha Scheme or Basic National Education. Its outstanding features were free compulsory education, craft as the centre of education, the mother tongue as the medium of instruction, and self-supporting education. Zakir Husain, a leading educationist, chaired a committee to work out the details of the programme and to produce a syllabus. Husain's committee reported in December 1937, and its report became the official Wardha Scheme. The plan was placed before the Indian National Congress at Haripura in February 1938, and received approval. The Congress, however, left out the notion that craft education should be self-supporting. An educational association, Hindustani Talimi Sangh, was established in 1939, to begin experimental schools and teacher training centres. Within a year schools began to spring up in Bombay, Bihar, Orissa, Uttar Pradesh and Madhya Pradesh.

The plan received an early setback in the 1940s due to the political climate and the difficulty in establishing it on a comprehehsive scale. Between 1940 and 1950, five All-India Educational Conferences were called to discuss, modify and advance

5. *Ashram Observances*, p. 3.

6. Patel, *The Educational Philosophy of Mahatma Gandhi*, p. 110.

the Wardha Scheme. At a Sevagram conference in 1945, Gandhi put before the country his entire scheme of pre-basic, basic, post-basic and adult education. Pre-basic education was designed for those under six years of age wherein the elementary principles of sanintation, hygiene, nutrition, work and helping parents in the home were introduced. Basic education was a seven-year plan from seven to fourteen. Post-basic education between fourteen and eighteen was an extension of the basic plan with a greater emphasis on self-sufficiency whereby the youth was to meet in craft education the expenses of food, clothing and education itself. University education followed with an orientation to national and social needs. Finally, adult education, a continuing programme was oriented to social service and community improvement. Again in 1947, Gandhi restated the principles of the Wardha Scheme and asked the nation to adopt it fully.

The Wardha Scheme drew negative criticism from the very beginning. Muslims opposed it for they saw it in opposition to Muslim culture due to the ideology of *ahiṃsā*. Yet the plan did not presuppose the acceptance of non-violence for one to support it.[7] Some argued that there was more non-violent sentiment in the plan than sound educational philosophy; others saw the teaching of academic subjects through a craft as simplistic.[8] The lack of qualified teachers was a familiar criticism even by those who had accepted the programme in principle. The fundamental criticism was its major emphasis on primary education, leaving secondary and higher education to a subordinate consideration. Gandhi's innovation here is unique. He did not intend higher education to change the course of primary education; higher education was to be the natural growth of what had already been learned in the early years. Gandhi's programme grew over the years. In Maharashtra in 1938, basic education was initiated provisionally in 55 schools of four different language families and expanded gradually over the years. By 1947-48 there were 524 Gandhian

7. *Basic Education*, p. 81.

8. See Patel, *The Educational Philosophy of Mahatma Gandhi*, p. 81 ; the plan was modified to teach a subject through a craft as far as possible.

schools, increasing to 2,816 in 1954-55, and 4,227 in 1961-62.[9] Spinning was the craft adopted in close to 3,000 of these schools, with agriculture and woodwork also being popular.

The Wardha Scheme still did not become a national programme of Indian education. Shriman Narayan observed that basic education in the final analysis was not given a fair hearing in India.[10] Some of the principles were easily accepted, but craft as the centre of education was not, either by educators or government. In 1956 the government appointed an assessment committee on basic education, but its recommendations favouring the Gandhian plan did not receive serious consideration. In a report from an educational seminar in Bombay in the early 1960s, craft was rejected as the medium of instruction in the first four years of school and were replaced with hobbies and play activities. Craft was introduced from the fifth to the eighth years and for three years only. This report reflected a general position against the correlation of craft and academic subjects.[11] Again in 1966, the Kothari Education Commission had its recommendations ignored. Yet as late as 1970 the Ministry of Education conducted a seminar at Sevagram on Gandhian education in which it upheld the principle of the "dignity of manual labour through the use of work as part of the educational programme."[12] But in the fourth Five Year Plan of the central government, no mention of basic education or work experience was made.

M.S. Patel and N.P. Pillai, supporters of Gandhian education, believe that the plan was really not tested on a national scale. Zakir Husain consistently criticized the direction of education in India and the failure to support the Gandhian plan. The fact remains that India today rejects much in Gandhi's conception of education, especially its notion of self-support and its emphasis on primary education in preference to higher education. Pandit Nehru, however, in following up the Wardha Scheme stressed industrial crafts (Bombay Plan)

9. *Seminar on Educational Reconstruction: Report* (Bombay: Gandhi Smarak Nidhi, 1963), pp. 44-46ff.
10. Narayan, *Towards Better Education*, p. 56.
11. *Seminar on Educational Reconstruction: Report*, pp. 65-69ff.
12. Narayan, *Towards Better Education*, p. 56.

in his conception of the plan as distinguished from agricultural work in the Wardha Scheme. Pillai, who made a thorough study of Gandhian education, concluded as far back as 1955 that "It may be seen that the scheme of basic education now accepted by the Government of India is not the same as the one which Gandhi had originally outlined."[13]

Today the *āsram* and centre at Sevagram remain the model and paradigm of Gandhi's dream. There is a small pre-school and basic school which follow the Gandhian programme quite exactly. It has the character of all that Gandhi envisioned. Surrounding the Sevagram Āśram is a vast network of craft industries sponsored and supported by the government, but the correlation of craft and learning is not at all apparent in this effort. In the Sevagram Āśram a living model remains which could inspire social reform in order to raise village life and consciousness. It offers to Indian educators perceptive alternatives for the future.

Gandhi visited Tagore's Santiniketan five times. Their admiration for each other was profound, and Gandhi always consulted Tagore before his major non-cooperation movements and public fasts. He referred to the poet as "Gurudev," and Tagore looked upon Gandhi as the singular "Mahatma." Yet as Pandit Nehru once remarked, no two people could be more different in character and life. In fact, they disagreed on every public issue of the day: civil disobedience, spinning and the burning of foreign cloth, approaches to Hindu-Muslim unity, birth control, morality and education. As early as 1915 Gandhi spoke to Tagore of the "behavioural shortcomings of Santiniketan" and suggested that Tagore's *āśram* would improve by adopting more discipline and directive principles of operation.[14] Tagore, on the other hand, objected to training in a craft for in his view it did not offer a creative world view to the young.

Tagore and Gandhi shared a fundamental understanding of Indian civilization. Both of them looked upon their contribution to education as their most significant legacy to this civili-

13. Pillai, *The Educational Aims of Mahatma Gandhi*, p. 295.

14. M. K. Gandhi, quoted in Sibnarayan Ray, edit., *Gandhi, India and the World, An International Symposium* (Bombay: Nachiketa Publications, Ltd., 1970), p. 111.

zation. They shared the common insight that education must be within a communal and natural context. Tagore considered education as a means for the development of a broad humanism; the religion of man was his stated goal. Gandhi, however, focused more upon character formation in the creation of a non-violent personality and a non-violent social order. Tagore found in creativity the purpose and meaning of human existence, and whatever contributed to the creative personality was for him good education. Gandhi considered *ahiṃsā* the goal and meaning of life, and whatever advanced truth and love was, consequently, good education. Tagore was motivated by the joy of truth and beauty in nature and in the created order among men; Gandhi was inspired by a comprehensive yet practical vision of a new social order. Tagore celebrated the body for its beauty, its joy and creation, while Gandhi looked to the body cautiously as an instrument of passion and a tool for service. As Tagore anticipated education to bring about an organic unity of man and the universe, Gandhi viewed education as more purposive and directive in the concrete order of things. The joy of life, the eternal *ānanda*, was the spirit of Tagore's schools; the disciplined pursuit of the higher levels of truth and non-violence was the character of Gandhian *āśrams*. Although both held broad horizons, Tagore was the supreme internationalist in early twentieth century India, whereas Gandhi remained the committed nationalist. Their educational theory and praxis reflected the specific spiritual character of their own personalities. Their educational systems, however, did not surpass them in greatness.

PART THREE

SRI AUROBINDO GHOSE

1872-1950

CHAPTER NINE

The Man: Psychic Personality

> To write my biography is impossible . . . Not only in my case but in that of poets, philosophers and Yogis, it is no use attempting a biography, because they do not live in their external life.[1]

Sri Aurobindo Ghose was a poet, philosopher and *yogi*. He

1. Sri Aurobindo, quoted in A.B. Purani, *The Life of Sri Aurobindo* (Pondicherry: Sri Aurobindo Ashram, 2nd edit., 1960), p. 235. Primary material on Sri Aurobindo's life are *Sri Aurobindo on Himself and on the Mother* (Pondicherry: Sri Aurobindo Ashram, 1958), *Correspondence with Sri Aurobindo*, comp. Nirodbaran (Pondicherry: Sri Aurobindo Ashram, 1969). The most definitive biography is K. R. Srinivas Iyengar, *Sri Aurobindo: A Biography and a History* (Pondicherry : Sri Aurobindo Ashram, 3rd rev. edit., 1972). Also helpful are: R.R. Diwakar, *Mahayogi Sri Aurobindo* (Bombay: Bharatiya Vidya Bhavan, 1967) ; Nolini Kanta Gupta, *Sri Aurobindo and His Ashram* (Pondicherry: Sri Aurobindo Ashram, 1948) ; Sisirkumar Mitra, *The Liberator: Sri Aurobindo, India and the Word* (Bombay: Jaico Publishing House, 1970) ; M.P. Pandit, *Reminiscences and Anecdotes of Sri Aurobindo* (Pondicherry: Sri Aurobindo Ashram, 1966) ; P.B. Saint-Hilaire (Pavitra), *The Message of Sri Aurobindo and His Ashram* (Pondicherry: Sri Aurobindo Ashram, 1947) ; Satprem, *Sri Aurobindo: or The Adventure of Consciousness* (Pondicherry : Sri Aurobindo Ashram, 1968), trans. by Tehmi.

cautioned biographers and even his own disciples that "Neither you nor anyone else knows anything at all of my life; it has not been on the surface for men to see."[2] Yet he approved some of his biographers and read others with great amusement. The biographies disclose two important factors. First, his life was a result of powerful psychic experiences which advanced steadily in quality and quantity throughout the years. Secondly, his psychic experiences were closely interwoven with the particular activity in which he found himself whether growing into manhood, engaged in politics, poetics, or philosophy, or involved in the spiritual direction of his disciples and *āśram*. The life of Aurobindo Ghose is a saga of psychic experiences and what these experiences do to a man and where they take him.

He was born on August 15, 1872, in the town of Konnagar, eleven miles north of Calcutta in the Hooghly district. The Ghoses were originally a Punjabi family, and by the time of Aurobindo's birth his father, Krishnadhan, had become a respected medical doctor known for his generosity and magnanimity. The young Aurobindo was the third of five children, four boys and a girl. His father who had done graduate work in medicine at Aberdeen University gave his children Western education and sent the five year old Aurobindo to Darjeeling to a convent school run by Irish nuns where his companions were British and English was the medium of instruction. As a child in Darjeeling, Aurobindo Ghose had his first psychic experience, an experience of oppression that stayed with him for fifteen years:

> I was lying down one day when I saw suddenly a great darkness rushing into me and enveloping me and the whole universe. After that I had a great *tamas* always hanging on to me all through my stay in England. I believe that darkness has something to do with the *tamas* that came upon me.[3]

The Ghose family went to England in 1879 when Aurobindo was seven. The three Ghose boys were placed in an English

2. Quoted in Iyengar, *Sri Aurobindo*, Vol. 1. p. 34.,
3. Quoted in Purani, *The Life of Sri Aurobindo*, pp. 6-7.

family, whom Dr. Ghose gave instructions that the boys were neither to enter into Indian friendships nor be influenced by anything Indian. The two older boys were sent to a Manchester school, but Aurobindo was tutored privately by Reverend William Drewett, a Congregational minister, the head of the family in which the boys lived. He was introduced to Latin, English and French, the writings of Keats, Shelley and Shakespeare, and the whole range of classical learning. In 1884 the Drewetts moved to London with the Ghose boys, and Aurobindo matriculated at St. Paul's School where he began writing poetry at seventeen and saw this as his future vocation. He quickly won a scholarship to King's College, Cambridge. By this time he read and spoke English and French fluently, and also read and wrote Greek and Latin with ease. He won various academic prizes at Cambridge where his tastes ranged from literature, especially poetry, to history and politics, but not philosophy. The Irish revolutionary Charles Parnell became a fav ourite. At Cambridge he met many Indians and began to learn Bengali; he took part in the debates of the Indian Majlis and participated in a group called "The Lotus and Dagger," a secret society the members of which took vows committing themselves to Indian independence. He became a candidate for the Indian Civil Service, passed the examination, but failed to take a required riding test, probably because he was trying to eliminate the Civil Service as a future career. There are some hints of spiritual experiences in 1892 in England, but he left for India in December of that year arriving to find that his father had just died.

The second extraordinary experience took place upon Aurobindo's arrival in India at the Bombay Gate. He described it as a "vast calm" that descended upon him and surrounded and remained with him for months afterwards.[4] Recalling this moment of calm as the lifting of the heavy darkness that had been with him for fifteen years, he wrote some years later to a disciple:

> ...since I set foot on the Indian soil on the Apollo Bunder in Bombay, I began to have spiritual experiences, but these

4. *Sri Aurobindo on Himself and on the Mother*, p. 84.

> were not divorced from this world but had an inner and infinite bearing on it, such a feeling of the Infinite pervading material space and the Immanent inhabiting material objects and bodies. At the same time I found myself entering supraphysical worlds and planes with influences and an effect from them upon the material plane . . .[5]

Aurobindo went to Baroda where he was to remain for the next thirteen years in the Baroda State Service in administrative work, in departments of revenue and land settlements, and in part-time teaching. He became a confidential adviser and sometime secretary to the Maharaja of Baroda before accepting a post as professor at Baroda College in 1900.

In Baroda Aurobindo immersed himself in the Indian heritage. He studied Bengali literature, Sanskrit, Marathi and Gujarati, and was soon able to read the *Mahābhārata* the *Rāmāyaṇa* and modern Bengali literature. Along with these literary activities he appeared on the political scence by writing anonymous articles in *Indu Prakash*, a Bombay journal of the Nationalist Party, entitled "New Lamps for Old." The articles brought him to the attention of Lokamanya Tilak, the Nationalist leader, but they were immediately opposed by Ranade, the leader of the moderates. In his early political writing, he tried to prod Indians, especially fellow Bengalis, to emerge from their sentimentalism over past history and to react politically to the British colonialists. From the turn of the century, he was drawn more and more into revolutionary politics and formed a secret political organization. In 1904 and 1905, he was a spokesman and leader of the Nationalists at the meetings of the Congress Party, The Nationalist platform was "Swarāj-Swadeshi-Boycott," the identical issues he had identified in his first political writing. In "Bhavani Mandir" written in 1903, he had sown the germ of the Hindu revolutionary movement in Bengal by giving an ultimatum to the British. With a sword and *Gītā* in hand, pledging to secure freedom for India, Aurobindo established six centres for revolutionary workers in Bengal.

5. Sri Aurobindo, *On Yoga*, II, Tome One (Pondicherry: Sri Aurobindo Ashram, 1958), p. 129.

He married Mrinalini Bose in 1901. It is a marriage difficult to understand because of the long periods of separation between the couple due to both Aurobindo's political and spiritual activities. Although he expressed in letters a touching affection toward his wife, partial separation took place at the height of his political activity in Calcutta and a total separation finally occurred in 1910. She died in 1918 at an early age.

In the first fifteen years in India, Aurobindo wrote close to 25,000 lines of verse. He wrote creatively and journalistically, both verse and prose. Translations from Bengali poetry and Sanskrit, plays, long narrative poems and short philosophical poems were added to a growing number of political essays. His narrative poem, *Urvasie*, appeared in 1896, and was soon followed by *Love and Death*, an epic romance. His first play was *Perseus the Deliverer*, somewhat Shakespearean in verse, and this was followed by five more plays and some unfinished ones. Aurobindo was drawn early to the Sanskrit poet *Kalidāsa* and the English and Irish poets; he believed that the aesthetic faculties had advanced the evolution of man more than anything else because they had refined and elevated emotions, heart and imagination to an intellectual level.

During these final years in Baroda, as he became more involved in politics, he began *yoga*. He was at first not attracted to *yoga* for he saw it as a retreat from life, but as he sought the strength to succeed in politics he began sustained *prāṇayama* (breathing techniques). The effect was immediate. Not only did he acquire new energy for politics but also greater mental clarity in his literary work. At one point he was doing three hours of *prāṇayama* in the morning and another two hours in the evening. His health improved, his memory became sharper, and an unprecedented flow of poetry resulted. He was able to write sometimes close to two hundred lines of verse in less than an hour. Aurobindo experienced *darśan* from Swami Brahmananda in 1903, an experience which overwhelmed him. Moreover, while in Kashmir near the Śaṅkara temple, he had a mysterious experience described as "one strange Unnameable,/ An unborn sole Reality world-nude,/ Topless and fathomless,/ a lonely Calm and void unchanging Peace."[6] Also, an experi-

6. Quoted in Iyengar, *Sri Aurobindo*, Vol. II, p. 679.

ence of Kali in a Karnali temple near Chandod was described as "A living Presence. deathless and divine,/ The great World-Mother/ Voiceless, inscrutable, omniscient."[7] A few years previously in avoiding a carriage accident he had the experience of being protected by a "Being of Light."

With the partition of Bengal by the British, Aurobindo withdrew from Baroda and began open participation in the turbulent politics of Calcutta and the nation. He saw it as "The Hour of God," the title of an article on Indian freedom and colonialism:

> There are moments when the Spirit moves among men and the breath of the Lord is abroad upon the waters of our being . . . when even a little effort produces great results and changes destiny . . . it is the hour of the unexpected.[8]

He became the editor of *Bande Mataram*, one of the leading nationalist newspapers in India. He and Rabindranath Tagore were central in establishing a new National College in Calcutta, and Aurobindo became its first principal. Recognized as the leader of the Nationalists in Bengal between 1905 and 1910, he was one of the four national leaders, along with Tilak, Lajpat Rai and Bepin Chandra Pal. By 1906 the Nationalists were vigorously advocating *swadeshi*, boycott and national education, issues Aurobindo had raised in previous years. *Bande Mataram* became the voice of the movement as Aurobindo discussed the doctrine of passive resistance in which he advocated violence in some circumstances. Believing that the divine was calling him deeper and deeper into politics, he wrote to his wife in 1907: "I am no longer my own master; I will have to go like a puppet . . ."[9] He was hailed as the high priest of nationalism by the Bengalis. As early as 1907 Rabinbranath Tagore recognized Aurobindo's role in national life and wrote:

> O friend, my country's friend, O voice incarnate free . . .
> The fiery messenger that with the lamp of God

7. *Ibid.*, Vol. 11, pp. 679-80.
8. *Ibid.*, Vol. 1, p. 345.
9. *Ibid.*, Vol. 1, p. 395.

Hath come—
Bursting its rock cage,—the voice of thunder deep . . .
Rabindranath,
O Aurobindo,
bows to thee.[10]

Tilak in Maharashtra had nationalized politics, but Aurobindo in Bengal began to spiritualize it. In his essays he went to the Indian religious tradition for parallels and metaphors to draw a lesson for nationalism. He based nationalism upon religious creed and was able to say that "Nationalism is a religion that has come from God."[11] India was the Mother, the *śakti* (conscious energy) of the Supreme. Aurobindo was arrested by the British for his political activities, was quickly prosecuted and won acquittal. This publicity pushed him into the lime-light as a national political figure.

Aurobindo's *sādhana* continued and a type of severity appeared in his life style, clothing and eating habits. In 1907 at Surat, he met a Maharashtrian *yogi*, Vishnu Bhasker Lele, whom he invited to Baroda a year later. For three days Aurobindo left behind all public activity and was isolated with Lele in *sādhana*. Lele brought Aurobindo to a suspension of thought and mental activity, and he had his initial experience of the silent mind. This was the first transformative experience in Aurobindo's life:

> . . . in three days I was free. From that moment, in principle, the mental being in me became a free Intelligence, a universal Mind, not limited to the narrow circle of personal thought . . .but a receiver of knowledge from all the hundred realms of beings and free to choose what it willed.[12]

From this point onward, he continued in politics and literary work as if his activity and his knowledge were given to him. Having overcome the ego, Aurobindo called it his *nirvanic*

10. Rabindranath Tagore, *Sri Aurobindo Mandir Annual* (1944), pp. 2-3, quoted in Iyengar, *Sri Aurobindo*, Vol. 1, p. 414.
11. Sri Aurobindo, *Speeches* (Pondicherry : Sri Aurobindo Ashram, 3rd ed., 1952), p. 55, quoted in Iyengar, *Sri Aurobindo*, Vol. 1, p. 477.
12. *Sri Aurobindo on Himself and on the Mother*, p. 133.

experience. He severed the ties with Lele when he discovered the presence of the inner *guru* to whom he could surrender completely. In the middle of this same year, Aurobindo was arrested in connection with the the Muzafapore bomb activity. With several dozen other revolutionaries he was imprisoned in the Alipore Jail for almost a year as the trial dragged on. Aurobindo began a year of silent *sādhana*, *prāṇayama*, fasting, prayer and meditation, and experienced the presence of a silent mind within his jail cell. Extraordinary experiences multiplied: occult happenings and levitations, a vision of Vivekananda teaching him for fifteen days, visions of *Nārāyaṇa*, *Vāsudeva* and other Hindu gods, experiences of universal love and peace. In the Alipore Jail, Aurobindo was psychically changed. It was the first of the triple transformations that would eventually take place. He did not negate his previous experiences, for he observed that "From the beginning I didn't feel Nirvana to be the highest spiritual achievement." The basic accomplishment of his Alipore transformation was that "the truth of the Supermind was put into me."[13] Aurobindo was acquitted with fifteen others in early 1909, and he realized that after a year in jail he had been totally transformed as a man. Because of his meditations on the *Gītā* in prison, he left as a *karma-yogin*, a worker of the divine.

He immediately began two new newspapers, *Karmayogin* in English and *Dharma* in Bengali, with articles by himself on education, translations of the *Upaniṣads*, poems and essays, and rather guarded political pieces. As he tried to apply his new vision and *yoga* to life, persistent rumours circulated that he was marked for another arrest because of the seditious materials he was publishing. By February 1910, a warrant for his arrest was imminent, and he received on the eve of the arrest an *ādeśa*(inner divine command), "Go to Chandernagore," a French territory a few hours from Calcutta. Leaving abruptly and setting up residence in Chandernagore, Aurobindo entered fully into *sādhana* receiving more visions and experiences of occult worlds. He remained for one month before another *ādeśa* came to him, "Go to Pondicherry." He and his compa-

13. Nirodbaran, *Talks with Sri Aurobindo* (Pondicherry: Sri Aurobindo Ashram, 1966), pp. 211-12.

nions fled to Pondicherry, a French town south of Madras on the Bay of Bengal, and exiled themselves, along with other politicians under seige. Aurobindo chose Pondicherry because it was far from the oppression of Calcutta, yet still part of the Indian subcontinent. He remained there for the rest of his life.

Although many attempts were made to extradite Sri Aurobindo with offers of political asylum, he began the practice of *yoga* and the mystical life, along with the gradual articulation of his experience and the building of a spiritual community. He was politically silent both in word and action and was not to break his political silence until the 1940s. The first four years in Pondicherry became years of solitude in which he attempted through *yoga* to bring down spiritual powers into his physical being. Occasional visitors would come to the recluse in Pondicherry, one of whom, M. Paul Richard, as early as 1910, was impressed by Sri Aurobindo as an accomplished religious personality. Richard came again in 1914, this time with his wife, Mira, who was later to become the Mother of the *āśram*, and he convinced Sri Aurobindo of the need to begin a new journal, *Arya*, in English with a French counterpart. From 1914 to 1921, all of Sri Aurobindo's major philosophy was written and published in *Arya* each month.

Sri Aurobindo became the philosopher, a task new to him:

> Let me tell you in confidence that I never, never, never was a philosopher—although I have written philosophy. . . I knew precious little about philosophy before I did the Yoga and came to Pondicherry—I was a poet and politician, not a philosopher! How I managed to do it and why ?. . . my theory was that a Yogi ought to be able to turn his head to anything, I could not very well refuse.. .I had to write down in the terms of the intellect all that I had observed and come to know in practising Yoga daily, the philosophy was there automatically. . . [14]

Three major works were written simultaneously and published serially in *Arya: The Life Divine*, *The Synthesis of Yoga* and

14. Quoted in Dilip Kumar Roy, *Sri Aurobindo Came to Me* (Bombay: Jaico Publishing House, 1964), p.33.

The Ideal of Human Unity. *The Life Divine* is a systematic exposition of Sri Aurobindo's philosophy; *The Synthesis of Yoga* is both a theoretical and practical statement on integral *yoga;* and *The Ideal of Human Unity* sets the path and goals for both personal, cosmic and universal evolution. Also during these years he wrote and published in *Arya*, *Essays on the Gita*, *The Secret of the Veda*, *The Future Poetry* and *The Human Cycle*, plus numerous essays on Indian culture. By 1920 his major books had been complcted, all within a period of six years. During this period, he would be engaged in four or five books at one and the same time.

In 1914 Mira Alfassa Richard came to Pondicherry for a year's stay. Born in Paris in 1878, she was a sensitive youth, a visionary by the age of twelve, who had studied occultism with a master in Algeria for some time. Coming to Pondicherry by train, she had a vision of light emerging from the French colony. In her first meeting with Sri Aurobindo, she recognized him as the Kṛṣṇa of her visions and surrendered completely to him as *guru*. A spiritual relationship was established and a psychic collaboration began which continued for thirty-six years. Returning to Paris the following year, she kept up a five year corresdondence with him on her *sādhana*. From 1916 to 1921, she was in Japan with her husband and had several visits with Tagore who was then travelling in the Far East. Tagore asked Mira Richard to come to Santiniketan to head the new international university, Visva-Bharati. She, however, declined and returned to Pondicherry in 1921 to remain there permanently. By the following year she had taken over Sri Aurobindo's household and began teaching his disciples the meaning of discipleship and the significance of the *guru*. She and Sri Aurobindo worked collaboratively on their *sādhana*. Gradually she became accepted and recognized as the Mother of the *āśram* and the Mother of Sri Aurobindo's spiritual ascent. Sri Aurobindo made it explicit in time that he followed his *yoga* through the Mother, Mira Richard:

> The Mother's consciousness and mine are the same, the one Divine Consciousness in two, because that is necessary for the play. Nothing can be done without her knowledge and force, without her consciousness—if anybody really feels

her consciousness, he should know that I am there behind it and if he feels me it is the same with hers.[15]

On the other hand, the Mother, Mira Richard, had the same perception: "Without him, I exist not; without me, he is unmanifest."[16] In Indian terms the Mother was the manifestation of *śakti*, the conscious force in the world process raising and advancing the evolution of the created cosmos.

In the early 1920s while Sri Aurobindo was testing his *yoga* on the physical plane, the atmosphere of the *āśram* was spiritually charged with anticipation of another transformation in him. The disciples and the Mother would gather around Sri Aurobindo in the early evening for meditation and conversation. His talks to them concentrated on supramental *yoga*. At the beginning of the Pondicherry exile, he had experienced the descent of mind to matter and the ascent of mind to supermind. Yet all was sporadic and temporary for there was no integration of the levels of reality, no linking of the processes whereby the experiences could be stabilized. For the ascent not to be disengaged from the world, integration with the world and the physical had to be made. When he commenced *The Life Divine*, Sri Aurobindo had already discovered the power and the principle of the higher mind, Supermind, and this called for a new *yoga*, an effort totally in consciousness, which he worked out from 1914 to 1926. The second of the triple transformations was imminent and there was expectancy in the *āśram* in 1926. On November 24, 1926, the event took place. When the disciples assembled that evening, the *guru* emerged as a new man. No word was spoken, but when Sri Aurobindo and the Mother left the meditation that evening, one disciple, a woman, quietly announced, "The Lord has descended into the physical today."[17] Sri Aurobindo had attained integral consciousness. For the past years he and the Mother had attempted to verify the powers of

15. *Sri Aurobindo on Himself*, Vol. XXVI, Sri Aurobindo Birth Centenary Library (Pondicherry: Sri Aurobindo Ashram, 1972), p. 455.
16. The Mother, *The Mother on Sri Aurobindo* (Pondicherry: Sri Aurobindo Ashram, 1961), p. 1.
17. Quoted in Iyengar, *Sri Aurobindo*, Vol.11, p. 988.

consciousness and to test these powers had been their major work up to November 1926. With the descent of the Overmind in Sri Aurobindo, as the event was called, a new and higher consciousness operated in the physical and a new phase began in the life of the Pondicherry mystic. The Mother understood the event of the descent in this way:

> What Sri Aurobindo represents in the world of history is not a teaching, not even a revelation, it is a decisive action direct from the Supreme . . . Sri Aurobindo incarnated in a human body the supramental consciousness and has not only revealed to us the nature of the path to follow and the method of following it so as to arrive at the goal, but has also by his own personal realization given us the example; he has provided us with the proof that the thing can be done and the time is now to do it.[18]

Sri Aurobindo went into complete silence in 1926, broken only for the occasional visitor, and only hints remain of his life from this point onward. The Mother became the administrator of the *āśram* and the spiritual director of the disciples. Sri Aurobindo became the Witness behind the scenes as the Mother stepped forward to manifest his consciousness and his will. The master wrote letters to his disciples instructing them in integral *yoga*, and frequently the number of letters and notes rose to a hundred a day. He appeared publicly, but silently, to the disciples on *darśan* days, three or four celebrations a year. For a year or so following the event of the descent, the *āśram* was filled with extraordinary and unusual happenings, the expression of vision and miracle was everywhere. Sri Aurobindo called for an end to the occult phenomena by reorientating the *āśram* and told everyone, even the Mother, to concentrate on the physical and vital levels of life, to become *karma-yogins*. Tagore visited the sage in 1928 and recognized the transformation:

> You have the Word and we are waiting to accept it from you. India will speak through your voice to the world. . . . Years ago I saw Aurobindo in the atmosphere of his earlier

18. *The Mother on Sri Aurobindo*, p.1.

> heroic youth and I sang to him, 'Aurobindo, accept the salutation from Rabindranath.' Today, I saw him in a deeper atmosphere of a reticent richness of wisdom and again sang to him in silence. 'Aurobindo, accept the salutation from Rabindranath.'[19]

During the silent years, Sri Aurobindo spent twelve hours a day writing, from six in the evening to six in the morning, and the following eight hours for *yoga*, walking up and down within his quarters. He revised *The Life Divine* and *The Synthesis of Yoga*, adding to the former a section on the Overmind. He continued to write poetry, doing experiments on metre, but now his poetry was inspired by a new mind. Having completed his philosophical work, he devoted himself to the epic poem *Savitri: A Legend and a Symbol*, a work of 23,800 lines of iambic blank verse. *Savitri* became the primary literary work for the last thirty years of his life. The epic poem took fifty years in the process, thirty years of concentrated writing, and began to appear in print only in 1946, with the complete text in 1951, a year after his death. It was poetry from a *yogic* consciousness which became for him a field of experimentation, for he said, "I used *Savitri* as a means of ascension."[20] Sri Aurobindo saw English verse approximating the Indian *mantra*, and *Savitri* was an attempt to achieve in English something analogous to the Vedic *mantra*, whereby both words and rhythms are symbolic. The basis of the poem is the Savitri-Satyavan story in the *Mahābhārata* wherein the legend becomes a symbol. So too *Savitri* is both legend and symbol; it possesses a double time and double action. The legend comprises historical time in the life and experiences of Sri Aurobindo and the Mother and also is symbolic of all eternity; its action recalls poetically the experiences of Sri Aurobindo and the Mother and also is symbolic of action within the soul of humanity. It is the life of Sri Aurobindo and the Mother unfolding in poetry, in twelve books of forty-nine cantos. *Savitri* is not

19. Rabindranath Tagore, *Sri Aurobindo and Rabindranath Tagore* (Pondicherry: Sri Aurobindo Ashram, 1961), p. 12, quoted from *Modern Review* (1928).

20. *Mother India*, Vol. VIII, N. 8 (Sept. 1956), pp. 4-5.

only the theory and knowledge of *yoga*, but it is also a manual of *yoga*. It can be a *sādhana*, a *yoga* in reading and understanding. It is the poetic counterpart of *The Life Divine*, written in the 1910s. In the 1930's Sri Aurobindo worked principally on *Savitri*, writing, making corrections, additions, rearrangements and recasting whole parts of the original due to his growth in consciousness.

In 1938, due to a fractured leg resulting from an accidental fall, Sri Aurobindo resumed conversations with his disciples. Not only spiritual matters but literature, art, politics, education, psychology, religion and war were discussed. The *āśram* grew in these years, adding men and women and in time, children. It was not a typical Indian *āśram*, for it was modern, scientific, and it brought together a multiplicity of types at various levels of spiritual progress. From the beginning it was seen as a place not for renouncing the world but for evolving a new being in the world. With the Second World War, Sri Aurobindo broke his political silence and actively supported the Allies. India gained independence on August 15, 1947, the seventy-fifth birthday of the *guru*. He saw it as no coincidence but as "the sanction and seal of the Divine Force that guides my steps on the work with which I began my life, the beginnings of its full fruition."[21] In 1949 he began a series of articles, some experiential and others merely speculative, on the "Mind of Light," a new power which illuminates the mind-body of the transformed man.

Sri Aurobindo became afflicted with uraemia and on December 5, 1950 died. He was not burried immediately as was the custom because of the luminosity of his body and the fact that decomposition did not begin until a hundred hours after his death. In subsequent years, the Mother continued the *āśram* for his work was not done. Sri Aurobindo had experienced the supramental in himself in 1926 and worked until his death to stabilize the new conciousness in the world. But it was only in 1956 that the Mother experienced it in the earth consciousness, thus completing the triple transformation of Sri Aurobindo's *yoga*. Announcing the February 29, 1956, event a month later, she said:

21. *Sri Aurobindo on Himself and the Mother*, pp. 246-247.

> The manifestation of the Supranatural upon earth is no more a promise but a living act, a reality. It is at work here, and one day will come when the most blind, the most unconscious, even the the most unwilling shall be obliged to recognize it.[22]

A psychic journey had reached fulfilment.

22. Quoted in Iyengar, *Sri Aurobindo*, Vol. 11, p. 1369.

CHAPTER TEN

His Thought: Integral Yoga

An experienced integralism is Sri Aurobindo's starting point in his comprehensive philosophical system. His massive but consistent philosophical writing is a result of reflection on psychic experience and, especially, reflections from the silent mind over a fifty year period. "*The Life Divine* is not philosophy but fact. It contains what I have realized and seen," said Aurovindo some years after completing the work.[1] The experienced unicity of divine and cosmic existence makes integralism a possibility and a necessity in his system. Integral philosophy attempts to unite categories of existence through *yoga*, for he observed:

> I had no urge to spirituality in me, I developed spirituality. I was incapable of understanding metaphysics, I developed into a philospher. I had no eye for painting—I developed it by yoga, I transformed my nature from what it was to what it was not. I did it by a special manner not by a

1. Sri Aurobindo, *Reminiscences and Anecdotes of Sri Aurobindo,* p. 10. The basic philosophical writings of Sri Aurobindo are found in the following volumes of the Centenary Library (Pondicherry: Sri Aurobindo Ashram, 1972) : Vol. 15, *Social and Political Thought* ; Vol. 16, *The Supramental Manifestation*; Vol. 18, 19, *The Life Divine*; Vol. 20, 21, *The Synthesis of Yoga*; Vol. 22, 23, 24, *Letters on Yoga.*

> miracle and I did it to show what could be done and how it could be done.[2]

His occult cosmology and metaphysics reflects both a developed spirituality and an experienced philosophy.

Ignoring brevity but with repetitive and circular prose, Sri Aurobindo created a new philosophical vocabulary to articulate and to systematize his psychic growth beginning with his first major experience in the Alipore Jail and his meditations on the *Bhagavad Gītā* and the *Upaniṣads*. He believed that the highest truths were already contained in the Vedas with the *Gītā* and *Upaniṣads* being a logical continuation of the ancient Vedas. His system included the fourfold *yoga* of the *Gītā*, that is, the *yoga* of knowledge (*jñāna*), the *yoga* of devotion (*bhakti*) the *yoga* of activity (*karma*), and the yoga of concentration (*dhyāna*). His thought included structures from the *Śāṇkhya* system, Patañjali's *yoga* and classical Vedānta. Accepting from the *Gītā* both the fourfold *yoga* and the notion of divine descent (*avatār*), he derived also from it his understanding of the *karma-yogin*:

> The central ethical injunction of the Gītā—'Fixed in yoga do thy actions' (11, 48)—this freedom is that yoga of the *Gītā*. When the interior joys and sorrows, instead of depending on external good and evil, well-being and danger become self-generated, self-propelled, self-bound, then the normal condition is reversed, and the outer life can be modelled on the inner, the bondage of action slackens.[3]

Sri Aurobindo's conception of man was consonant with much of traditional Indian thought. The essential divinity of man and the spiritual progress of the individual and society were readily assimilated from the tradition. He accepted from classical understanding union with the supreme and union with the

2. Nirodbaran, *Correspondence with Sri Aurobindo* (1969), p. 58, quoted in *The Essential Aurobindo*, edit. Robert McDermott (New York: Schocken Books, 1973), p. 19.
3. Sri Aurobindo, "Prison and Freedom," in *Kara Kahini*, trans. Sisirkumar Ghosh (Pondicherry: Sri Aurobindo Ashram, 1969), p. 158.

universal self as paramount. However, Sri Aurobindo differed from the past and from the *Gītā* in introducing *yoga* into full historical and cosmic life. In his view supramental life, the life of *yoga*, has for its aim the introduction of the divine into history. He saw this as differentiating his thought from the *Gītā*:

> The Gītā's *yoga* consists in the offering of one's work as a sacrifice to the Divine, the conquest of desire, egoless and desireless action, *bhakti* for the Divine, and entering into cosmic consciousness, the sense of unity with all creatures, oneness with the Divine. This *yoga* adds the bringing down of the supramental Light and Force (its ultimate aim) and the transformation of the nature.[4]

He looked for the middle path between the classical Indian ascetic who denied history or the visionary whose speculations were wholly futuristic on the one hand, and the materialist who was bound to the horizons of material existence on the other. Aurobindo sought a global synthesis of matter and spirit, a synthesis of the historical and the transhistorical, of the intellectual life and the supramental life, of material and spiritual transformation.

Integralism is possible in Sri Aurobindo's system through transformation. He integrated experience not through a forced juxtaposition of reatities and levels of being. Diverse principles and realities do not unite on their original level but are first transformed and then enter into a greater synthesis. For example, matter and spirit enter into synthesis only if matter loses its imperfections and limitations, but when it does so it can be integrated on a new level, a spiritual level, of being. The work of transformation is the work of man and the divine; transformation takes place most significantly on a supramental plane. What appears diverse is transformed and then integrated in such a way that unity and not opposition exists in the diversity. Sri Aurobindo got this perception of integration from the Hindu scriptures, and his interpretations of the

4. Sri Aurobindo, *Lights on Yoga* (Pondicherry: Sri Aurobindo Ashram, 1942), p. 89.

scriptures follow closely upon this principle. With the perception of integration through transformation, Aurobindo's philosophy became world-affirming, for it was neither an escape from historical processes nor salvation from rebirth. The spiritual process for Aurobindo is to overcome ignorance and the restrictions of the ego. The world is not illusion (*māyā*) as understood in much of the Hindu tradition but an inseparable power of the divine through which the latter manifests itself. Aurobindo is indebted to the Tantric tradition, especially, for that tradition's involvement in matter and the radical transformation of matter. He assimilated from Tantrism the insight that the universe and the historical process were inseparable from the supreme because they were expressions of divine energy. Transformation, leading to integration, is the rediscovery that the energy within the created universe is one with the divine. This influenced Aurobindo's philosophy of god, man, evolution, history and society.

Evolution in his system assures integration. Evolution is basically an evolution of consciousness wherein the relational forces from multiple and diverse levels of reality achieve unity. The three broad states of evolution commence with the movement from matter to life. That is, the raising of matter (the inconscient) to elementary levels of consciousness; secondly, the movement advances from life to mind, that is, the raising of ignorance to refined consciousness; and thirdly, the movement finally progresses from mind to Supermind, that is, the raising of man to supramental consciousness. The second level is man's place in history, but Sri Aurobindo's life work was basically on the third movement whereby man is transformed into a new being. The evolutionary spiral that Sri Aurobindo envisaged is a spiral of consciousness based upon his most radical claim that the inconscient when made conscious can achieve supramental existence. With the evolution of human consciousness, the evolutionary process attains self-consciousness. Hence the whole motive in evolution is growth in consciousness.

An experienced unity of the divine, which was Aurobindo's initial insight, reveals a structure of existence:

We perceive that our existence is a sort of refraction of the

Divine existence, in an inverted order of ascent, and descent, thus ranged,—

Existence	Matter
Consciousness-Force	Life
Bliss	Psyche
Supermind	Mind.[5]

Following a *Śāṇkhya* structure of reality, Sri Aurobindo worked out a basic cosmological category for the evolution of phenomena but a psychological category for the evolution of consciousness. The correspondence between the two keeps the process advancing. Man evolves both in terms of his outward nature and his inner being. A double process exists, one of involution and evolution, a descent and an ascent. It is necessary to understand involution first in Aurobindo's thought as the descent of pure consciousness to matter wherein matter is most essentially constituted as inconscient. This is creation. The spirit involves itself in matter and lower forms of life, and the whole of history then becomes the evolution of higher forms of life from the inconscient: first, lower forms of life, followed by animal life, and then culminating in human life. Evolution is ascent of reality from matter to consciousness, which indicates that Sri Aurobindo holds for no radical opposition between matter and spirit. In the evolutionary process, the higher levels of life are a manifestation and unfoldment of the spirit itself. There is, moreover, a double process at this moment for just as matter ascends to higher levels of life or man to higher levels of consciousness, so too mind descends to life and to matter and the supramental descends to mind. The absolute does not descend directly into the human mind or consciousness, but the mediation of the Supermind is necessary. Through Supermind, which is the divine in time and space, the Absolute descends to man and man rises to the Absolute.

Both Aurobindo and Hegel applied the principle of evolutionary integration to all existence, but in Aurobindo integration is wholly transformative. As the emergents such as matter,

5. Sri Aurobindo, *The Life Divine* (Pondicherry: Sri Aurobindo Ashram, 2nd impression, 1960), Vol. 1, p. 316.

life, animal consciousness, human self-consciousness evolve, each higher level lifts up, advances and transforms the lower level. When a lower level rises into a higher level, nothing is destroyed, dissipated or lost, but the lower level is infused, modified and radically transformed into a higher level of existence. Aurobindo's perception of man as a refraction of the divine implied a widening and a heightening in human and cosmic development. In widening the creative process, man and the cosmos differentiate by entering into variety and complexity, by descending and involuting into greater multiplicity and universality; at the same time in heightening the creative process, man develops and integrates stages and levels of life, resulting in a unicity and centering of the advancing ascent. Thus the process of evolution takes place through integration. When mind evolves it transforms and achieves unicity and integration without destroying its capacity for variety and multiplicity.

Aurobindo's basic perception, again, is that all reality is conscious and can be measured only by the level of consciousness revealed. The divine as Consciousness-Force is manifested outside itself. Consciousness-Force is the relational reality in the godhead which seeks manifestation. In the created order, vital energy (*śakti*) is within every name and form:

> We are each of us a dynamo into which waves of that energy have been generated and stored, and are being perpetually conserved, used up and replenished.[6]

The impetus in the evolutionary process is the power of pure supra-evolutionary existence.[7] Man must cooperate with this

6. Sri Aurobindo, *Integral Education*, comp. Indra Sen (Pondicherry: Sri Aurobindo International University Centre, 1952), p. 23.

7. See *The Integral Philosophy of Sri Aurobindo, A Commemorative Symposium*, edit. Haridas Chaudhuri & Frederic Spiegelberg (London: George Allen & Unwin, Ltd., 1960), p. 31. Helpful secondary works on the philosophy of Sri Aurobindo are: K.R. Srinivasa Iyengar, *Sri Aurobindo, An Introduction* (Mysore: Rao & Raghavan, 1961); A.B. Purani, *Sri Aurobindo's Life Divine* (Pondicherry: Sri Aurobindo Ashram, 1966); Nathaniel Pearson, *Sri Aurobindo and the Soul Quest of Man* (London: George Allen &

superconscient force (*śakti*) in order to achieve integral consciousness or integral personality or integral realization of ultimate reality. Man ascends to new being as he draws upon his psychic capacity, that is, the energy-force within him that makes him a high relational being. Salvation for Aurobindo is neither freedom from rebirth nor from the world process but rebirth of man as gnostic being, a supramental being. The purpose of evolution is the divinization of the individual and the cosmos, which takes place only with the gratuitous descent of Supermind, the highest integral experience for the individual. Supermind brings a decisive change in the nature of man which makes possible the new integral personality. Since the whole structure of man, his nature and destiny, is based on evolution, the transformation of man is achieved through the integral personality. But evolution is what makes integralism possible.

> Man is a transitional being; he is not final. For in man and high beyond him ascend the radiant degrees that climb to a divine supermanhood. There lies our destiny and the liberating key to our aspiring but troubled and limited mundane existence . . . Supermind is superman; a gnostic supermanhood is the next distinct and triumphant evolutionary step to be reached by earthly nature.[8]

Unwin, Ltd., 1952) ; Satprem, trans. by Tehmi, *Sri Aurobindo, the Adventure of Consciousness* (New York: India Library Society, 1964) ; Rhoda P. LeCocq, *The Radical Thinkers, Heidegger and Sri Aurobindo* (Pondicherry: Sri Aurobindo Ashram Press 1969); Paul Colaco, *The Absolute in the Philosophy of Aurobindo Ghose* (Rome: Pontificia Universitas Gregoriana, 1954) ; S.K. Maitra, *An Intraduction to the Philosophy of Sri Aurobindo* (Benares: Benares Hindu Undiversity, 1941) ; Ram Shankar Misra, *The Integral Advaitism af Sri Aurobindo* (Benares: Benares Hindu University, 1957) ; Anilbaran Roy, edit., *The Message of the Gita as Interpreted by Sri Aurobindo* (London: George Allen & Unwin,Ltd., 1946). Also see *Philosophy East-West*, Vol. XXII, No. 1 (January, 1972), and *International Philosophical Quarterlp*, Vol. XII, No. 2 (June, 1972).

8. *Handbook, Sri Aurobindo University Centre* (Pondicherry: Sri Aurobindo Ashram, 1953), p. 45.

Since the individual is a transitional being in Aurobindo's thought, man exceeds himself by conscious evolution. Sri Aurobindo's spiritual companion, the Mother, confirmed this: "Lord, we are upon earth to accomplish thy work of transformation. It is our sole will, our sole preoccupation."[9] Man's great adventure is the aspiration to transcend himself. Aspiration has been considered the most significant human phenomenon upon which Aurobindo's philosophy is based.[10] Man must aspire above what he is by conscious emerging, not through an escape from life but through conscious fulfilment of life. His first duty, according to Aurobindo, is to "affirm himself in the universe."[11]

Aurobindo's philosophy of man encompasses both a morphological and a genetic view of man. He described man morphologically in both cosmological and anthropological categories which gave a horizontal view of man's past, present and future. The genetic structure of man, which received greater emphasis, was described and systematized more speculatively in psychological categories and gave a vertical view of man's life. It is within the genetic-psychological structure that the meaning of mind, psyche and supramental being are discussed. The mind is the evolute of Supermind, limited in power and consciousness, created and derrivative, existing in ignorance and incapacity. The mind is raised in consciousness as ego is transcended. The basic experience consists in the descending force which integrates with the ascending aspiration and establishes something new in consciousness. Aurobindo drew upon the fundamental dynamic of Tantrism but reversed the process whereby the *cakras* (psychic openings) are opened from the top downward by the descending forces of consciousness and not from the bottom upward, as found in Tantrism with its violent opening of the psychic centres. Consciousness-Force is one of the basic constituents of the godhead along with Existence and Bliss. It is implicit and veiled in mind, life and matter but is not merely mind or mental consciousness.

9. *The Mother on Sri Aurobindo* (Pondicherry: Sri Aurobindo Ashram, 1961), p. 1.
10. See Jitendranath Mohanty, "Modern Philosophical Anthropology," *Sri Aurobindo Circle*, No. 12 (1960), p. 163.
11. *The Life Divine*, Vol. 11, Part 11, p. 815.

Consciousness-Force creates and involutes, evolves and manifests itself. For Aurobindo consciousness and force are somewhat interchangeable, but there is a marked difference between divine force and merely cosmic force. The evolutionary process and the higher evolution of man draw the divine Consciousness-Force into the created order in a powerful manner. This is accomplished through the triple transformation of man: psychic, spiritual and supramental.

The transformation of man begins with psychic change. Man's inner self is psychic being, according to Aurobindo: "This veiled psychic entity is the flame of the Godhead always within us, inextinguishable by that dense unconsciousness of any spiritual self within which obscures our outward nature."[12] Psychic being is the representative of the inner-self, the central being (*jīvātman*) which is spirit, the divine presence, the secret witness. A psychic personality is one whose inner-self controls the mind, life and body of the individual. A psychic personality takes a dynamic part in the activities and movements of his inner life. Psychic self-discovery is the means to change the lower nature of man since the psychic being exerts a force for transformation upon the lower nature. With psychic change, however, the person is not divinized, for this can only be accomplished through Supermind which continually descends and transforms man gradually through various spiritual stages to a divine status. Hence the realization of the psychic being is not total and final, but it is necessary for Supermind to enter gratuitously and fully for the supreme realization. According to Sri Aurobindo, "The psychic transformation after rising into the spiritual change has then to be completed, integralized, exceeded and uplifted by supramental transformation . . ."[13]

Spiritual transformation follows psychic change. In the ascent toward integral personality man must rise above himself through conscious aspiration and energization. There are four grades of spiritual transformation wherein the fields of existence are raised from Higher Mind to Illumined Mind to Intuition and, finally, to Overmind. The four grades of ascent

12. *The Life Divine*, (New York, 1949), Vol. 1, p. 207.

13. *The Life Divine*, (Pondicherry, 1960) Vol. 1, p. 273.

are the "energy of the spiritual being, fields of existence which are each a level of universal Consciousness-Force constituting and organizing itself into a higher status."[14] These overhead planes, as they were called by Aurobindo, influence the mental, the vital and the material levels of life. Sri Aurobindo spoke in his poetic criticism of the overhead consciousness which follows upon the spiritual awakening of man. The individual begins to perceive, for example, poetry or philosophy or art, from higher levels of consciousness. The final level in spiritual transformation is the descent of Overmind, the intermediary of Supermind, which gives universality to the individual. Aurobindo described this consciousness as

> . . . the final consummating movement of the dynamic spiritual transformation: it is the highest possible status-dynamic of the highest power, of the lower hemisphere; although its basis is a cosmic unity, its action is an action of division and interaction, an action taking its stand on the play of multiplicity.[15]

Overmind leads immediately into the third of the triple transformation, supramental change. The central concept in either human or cosmic evolution is, of course, Supermind. Supermind is the creative aspect of the godhead; it is god as lord and creator; it manifests some of the power of *Sachidānanda* (Existence, Consciousness-Force, Bliss) in the universe. Supermind is unfolded within man when he rises above mental consciousness and begins to live and to operate with a supramental consciousness. Although Supermind is a level of existence above man and his world, it still manifests itself in man and cosmos. The function of Supermind is to actualize and reveal *Sachidānanda*, the supreme, in the world. It overcomes dichotomous thinking, and the evolution of man and cosmos begin through knowledge. The personal effort of Sri Aurobindo was to initiate the conditions wherby Supermind could be a permanent state of consciousness in the world. The descent of Supermind initiates a radical change in the evolu-

14. *Ibid.*, Vol. 11, Part 11, p. 1116.
15. *Ibid.*, Vol. 11, Part 11, p. 1133.

tion of man; the age of gnostic man beginss. The new age of gnostic being brings also a radical change to the personality of man. According to Aurobindo:

> The gnostic consciousness will at once intimately and exactly know its object by a comprehending and penetrating identification with it. It will overpass what it has to know but it will include it in itself; it will know the object as part of itself . . ."[16]

Aurobindo's notion of salvation is the birth of a divine being, a superman, a gnostic being within man who has transcended ego, ignorance and human imperfection. Salvation is the perfection of the individual; it is a life divine. However, this does not bring an end to either human or cosmic destiny but issues in a new age of spiritual evolution. Sri Aurobindo did not anticipate all humanity rising to Supermind as a unit but only those whose inner evolution had prepared them to receive it. The influence of those who are of this consciousness touches all created life.

Integral *yoga* (*pūrṇa*) has for its object a distinct change of personality and existence as we now know it. Integral personality advances evolution. For Aurobindo, "What nature aims at for the mass in a slow evolution, *yoga* effects for the individual in a rapid evolution."[17] Integral *yoga* is the means to integral personality. It is not "to lose oneself in Divine Consciousness," wrote Aurobindo, but "to let the Divine Consciousness penetrate into Matter and transform it."[18] His *yoga* is directed toward the transformation of lower consciousness and subsequently the entrance into the divine life.

> The yoga we practice not for ourselves alone, but for the Divine, its aim is to work out the will of the Divine in the world, to effect a spiritual transformatian and to bring

16. *Ibid.*, Vol., 11, Part 11, p. 1170.
17. Sri Aurobindo, *On Yoga I*, *The Synthesis of Yoga* (Pondicherry: Sri Aurobindo Ashram, 1969), p. 269.
18. Sri Aurobindo, *The Destiny of Man* (Pondicherry: Sri Aurobindo Ashram, 1969), p. 269.

> down a divine nature and a divine life into the mental, vital and physical nature and life of humanity.[19]

In couse of time interal *yoga* creates the conditions for the descent of Supermind. It begins with the discovery of the divine in oneself, in society and in the cosmos. In *The Human Cycle* Aurobindo focused upon social and cosmic evolution with its concomitant *yoga*. There is a consistent balance in his system between meditation and activity, the *yoga* of the individual and the *yoga* of society; there is present the correlation of the ascending and descending movements of evolution and consciousness both in the individual and in society.

Aurobindo's integral *yoga* is not a fixed method of training in consciousness. His *yoga* operates freely, and the process accepts all that the individual is and capable of at a particular moment of life. There is neither a specific method nor a distinguishing mark to his *yoga*, for each individual has different starting points and to a great degree discovers his own method. Work is the basis of his *yoga*. Developing the notion of *karma-yoga* from the *Bhagavad Gītā*, Aurobindo believed that the individual "must have consciousness of the divine presence in . . . heart and the divine guidance in . . . acts."[20] In his *āśram*, work became the basis for all *sādhana*, and he stressed the *yoga* of work especially in the final twenty years with his disciples. In order to develop an integral *yoga* and an integral approach to the development of consciousness, Aurobindo insisted that "All life is yoga."[21] A yogic personality required integral life within the individual himself and the individual within society.[22] He drew again upon the Tantric thrust of involvement in matter and cosmos whereby energy (*śakti*) is the lord of *yoga*. For Aurobindo:

> It was by learning and applying the intimate secrets of this Will-in-Power, its method, its Tantra, that the Tantric yogin pursued the aims of his disciples,—mastery, perfection,

19. *Ibid.*, p. 245.
20. *Sri Aurobindo on Himself and on the Mother*, p. 707.
21. *On Yoga I, The Synthesis of Yoga* (1953), p. 4.
22. *On Yoga II*, Tome One (1958), p. 672.

> liberation, beatitude. Instead of drawing back from manifested Nature and its difficulties, he confronted them, seized and conquered.[23]

Man becomes an instrument of *śakti* in this system of *yoga*. Aurobindo stressed renunciation in work whereby activity is directed by the lord of *yoga*, and the fruits of activity are also left to the receptive *śakti*. Aurobindo saw this as a firmer base for *yoga* than either *hatha* or *rāja-yoga* (physical or mental), both practices which he considered useful but not entirely indispensable. *Hatha-yoga*, for instance, may produce good results "but at an exorbitant price and to very little purpose."[24] Physical *yoga* consumes time and energy and restricts an individual from full participation in the ordinary activity and affairs of social life. Likewise, *rājā-yoga* may well increase the individual's intellectual and mental capacities, but Aurobindo believed it was too dependent on abnormal states of trance, leading to a withdrawal from physical life. He said, "it tends to withdraw into a secondary plane at the back of our normal experiences instead of descending and possessing our whole existence."[25] Accordingly, *integrality* alone was the essential condition of Aurobindo's *yoga* for its goal was not just union with the divine but complete living in society in a spiritual way.

Aspiration and self-surrender received major emphasis in his practice of *yoga*. This particular focus is preceded by purification, concentration and meditation. For effective aspiration and surrender the heart must be concentrated to call upon the power of *śakti* to transform consciousness. Meditation is not thinking or imagining but "concentration or turning of the consciousness is important,—and that can happen in work, in writing, in any kind of action as well as in sitting down to contemplate."[26] Meditation or concentration through

23. *On Yoga I, The Synthesis of Yoga* (1965), p. 36.
24. *Ibid* , p. 29.
25. *Ibid.*, pp. 30-31.
26. Sri Aurobindo, *Letters of Sri Aurobindo* (Pondicherry: Sri Aurobindo Ashram, Fourth Series), quoted in Narayan Prasad, *Life in Sri Aurobindo Ashram*, (2nd edit., 1968), p. 33.

work and ordinary activities became a common practice in his *āśram*. Concentration opened one to the divine in order that aspiration and surrender would be effective. The singular mark of Aurobindo's praxis is aspiration and surrender. Aspiration is concentration inwards and upwards; surrender is the opening of self inwards and upwards to a deeper and higher consciousness. This can be achieved either in meditation or in work alone or jointly. It would seem that Sri Aurobindo achieved it principally in the act of writing. He observed that "to join with the true consciousness or feel its descent is the only thing important and if it comes without the orthodox method as it always did with me, so much the better."[27] He believed that if one had the capacity to surrender, "no other *tapasya* is needed."[28] Surrender and aspiration begin with the mind and heart and proceed to the vital being, which is the most difficult and resistant to relinquish. But all levels of man, all parts of his being have to be surrendered, even the psychic self in its movements and powers. The Mother said: "Surrender is the decision taken to hand over the responsibility of your life to the Divine . . . 'I do not belong to myself,' you say, and give up the responsibility of your being to the Truth. Then comes self-offering."[29] Once the surrender is complete, the full spiritual activity of the divine begins. Personal effort then is replaced by the divine activity taking up spiritual growth and elevating human consciousness by *śakti*, the divine Consciousness-Force. Aurobindo believed that the divine activity would enable the individual to "feel the presence of the divine in every centre of his consciousness, in every vibration of his life-force, in every cell of his body."[30] In this way integral *yoga* is directed toward the establishment of the life divine.

"The liberation and self-fulfilment of others is as much our own concern—we might almost say, our divine self-interest

27. *Ibid.*, p. 42.

28. *Ibid.*, p. 90.

29. *Words of the Mother* (Pondicherry: Sri Aurobindo Ashram, 3rd series, 1946), p. 6.

30. *The Life Divine* (1940), pp. 1035-36, quoted in Narayan Prasad, *Life in Sri Aurobindo Ashram*, p. 104.

—as our own liberation," wrote Aurobindo.[31] Integral *yoga* attempts to create the integral person, but integral personality is achieved only through a social and cosmic integralism. Aurobindo's *yoga* is in one way super-cosmic insofar as it is a total movement of life seeking knowledge; on the other hand, it is supra-terrestrial because it prepares for life on a completely new plane of existence; but the specificity of his *yoga* is earth-bound because it affirms life in society on earth through an activity-centered *yoga*. All three movements of the *yoga* must coexist for integralism. The entire universe and its societies ascend to higher levels of life with the aid of the self-realized individual. Sri Aurobindo envisaged cosmic salvation, much like Mahayana Buddhism, whereby the entire created order is spiritualized.

Few philosophers have been as confident of the future as Sri Aurobindo. He based this confidence upon the evolutionary process that he perceived in the social history of man. Observing progressive stages in social history, he called the first symbolic, an age of religion in which the first tendency toward subjective understanding appeared. The second stage was an age of ethics and psychology in which the tendency towards the refinement of the manner of living appeared. The third age was the time of conventional society which rejected formalism but accepted distinct patterns in life and thought; the fourth period was the time of individualism in society, an age of science and reason which returned society to a new subjectivity. This moment, which for Aurobindo is the present time in most societies, is a period of progress, freedom and revolution. But the coming society is the age of Supermind where the realization of god, freedom and unity will predominate in all social groups. In short, he envisaged a gradual spiritualization of society, a movement toward the life divine in the entire universe. In Aurobindo's social thought, society is determined by man and not man by society. He was more concerned with the goals and ideals of society than its institutions and practices. Unlike the cyclic patterns of history and society in traditional Indian thought, Aurobindo viewed history as spiral, a spiralling progression toward greater fulfil-

31. *On Yoga I, The Synthesis of Yoga* (1965), p. 6.

ment and perfection. Just as he builds his theory of evolution on a psychological approach to reality, so too his approach to history is subjective and psychological. The unity of the human race can only be achieved by integral living and through integral personality:

> The gnostic being finds himself not only in his own fulfilment, which is the fulfilment of the Divine Being and Will in him, but in the movement of others; his universal individuality effectuates itself in the movement of the All in all beings towards its greater becoming.[32]

The *yogin* realizes himself through the universe and through the historical processes in social life. Integral *yoga* is striving for spiritual change in society:

> There must be the individual and the individuals who are able to see, to develop, to recreate themselves in the image of the Spirit and to communicate both their idea and its power to the mass. And there must be at the same time a mass, a society, a communal mind or at least the constituents of a group-body, the possibility of a group-soul which is capable of receiving and effectively assimilating...[33]

An experienced integralism was Aurobindo's point of departure. He viewed integralism as possible only through transformation. Integral personality is discovered, created and developed both for personal man and for his society through *yoga*. Integral *yoga* which is the means to historical and cosmic transformation is fundamentally radical.

32. *The Life Divine* (New York: India Library Society, 1965), p. 913.
33. Sri Aurobindo, *The Human Cycle* (Pondicherry: Sri Aurobindo Ashram, 1962), pp. 330-32.

CHAPTER ELEVEN

Educational Theory

Sri Aurobindo articulated his basic educational ideas in the early part of the century when he addressed himself to the problem of national education. He called for an education that was as comprehensive as that found in Europe but far more thorough than it. Education, he believed, must offer the tools whereby one can live for the divine, for country, for oneself and others, and this "must be made the ideal in every school which calls itself national."[1] In *The Human Cycle* he identified the spiritual orientation of education and society:

1. Sri Aurobindo, *A Scheme of Education*, edit. Pranab Kumar Bhattacharya (Pondicherry: Sri Aurobindo Ashram), p, 47. Several good compilations of Sri Aurobindo and the Mother on education are: *Sri Aurobindo and the Mother on Education* (Pondicherry: Sri Aurobindo Ashram, 1956) ; *Sri Aurobindo and the Mother on Physical Education* (Pondicherry: Sri Aurobindo Ashram, 1967) ; *Integral Education, In the Words of Sri Aurobindo and the Mother*, comp. Indra Sen (Pondicherry: Sri Aurobindo International University Centre, 1952) ; *The Brain of India* (Pondicherry: Sri Aurobindo Ashram, 1967) ; *Sri Aurobindo and the Mother on Education*, Part I, *Education, General Principles*, Part II, *Education, Teaching*, Part III, *Education, Learning* (Pondicherry: Sri Aurobindo Society, 1972). Also helpful are journals published by the Sri Aurobindo Ashram, *Mother India, The Advent, Sri Aurobindo Mandir Annual* (Calcutta), *Handbook: Sri Aurobindo University Centre, Equals One, Bulletin of Physical Education*.

> ...the coming of a spiritual age must be preceded by the appearance of an increasing number of individuals who are no longer satisfied with the normal intellectual, vital and physical existence of man, but perceive that a greater evolution is the real goal of humanity and attempt to effect it in themselves, to lead others to it, and to make it the recognized goal of the race.[2]

Both society and education should provide the conditions for all men to "travel towards divine perfection" and to express the power, the harmony, the beauty and joy of self-realization that has been attained.[3] Criticizing systems of education which begin with an insufficient knowledge of man, especially systems supplying just information, Sri Aurobindo called for the study of the instruments of knowledge in a way that was natural, effective and complete. Since the individual and society grow in and through each other, education must be "the instrument for this real working of the spirit in the mind and body of the individual and the nation."[4] The guiding principle and orientation of Aurobindo's educational thought is the awakening of man as a spiritual being. He believed that neither education nor religion in the past had really changed man perceptibly and that a total spiritual orientation had now to be given to the whole of education and the life of the nation.

Since the principal instrument of knowledge is the mind, education must study the mental powers and processes. Sri Aurobindo pointed to the mind as the goal of education: "The true basis of education is the study of the human mind. infant, adolescent and adult."[5] Education must take account not only of the mind of the individual and the people but also the mind of the nation and of the universe. The major achievement of education, according to Aurobindo,

> . . . is the building of the powers of the human mind and spirit, it is the formation or, as I would prefer to view it,

2. *The Human Cycle*, p. 353.
3. *Ibid.*, p. 78.
4. *Education, General Principles*, p. 2.
5. *Integral Education*, p. 5.

> the evoking of knowledge and will and of the power to use knowledge, character, culture—that at least if no more.[6]

Because man is capable of further development, a conviction which was the basis of ancient Aryan education, true education in our day should bring out in man "the right relation" with the mind and soul of humanity.[7] Education involves man, nation and all humanity, because before the individual can grow there must be some change and reorientation on the collective level. Only that education which studies the mind can initiate this change in man and his society. In the Aurobindian school, the student is made aware that he was created to become a mental being. His goal is the growth of the human soul, the self, in all its powers and potentialities.

Sri Aurobindo founded the Pondicherry *āśram* as "a centre and a field of practice for the evolution of another kind and form of life" which would be sustained by a higher consciousness and embody a full life of the spirit.[8] The principles of his educational theory are similar and frequently the same as the principles of integral *yoga*. The first is the discovery and knowledge of the powers, principles and process of self-realization; the second is a patient and persistent personal effort in growth and change; the example and influence of the teacher is a further principle; and finally, the instrumentality of time undergirds all the principles. The first, the evolution of man in consciousness, begins with self-knowledge, a consciousness of the different parts of one's being. The Mother called self-mastery as the finest gift given to a child:

> To know oneself means to know the motives of one's actions and reactions, the why and the how of all that happens in oneself. To master oneself means to do what

6. *Sri Aurobindo and the Mother on Education*, p. 4.
7. *Integral Education*, p. 1.
8. *Mother India*, Special Issue for the Silver Jubilee of the Sri Aurobindo International Centre of Education, Vol. XX, No. 10-11 (Nov.-Dec., 1968) p. 4.

> one has decided to do, to do nothing but that, not to listen or to follow impulses, desires, or fancies.[9]

To know oneself is to observe and to develop the whole intellectual, moral and emotional complex of the personality. Self-development is an integral growth of the individual personality. For Aurobindo this is attempted through the development of the four austerities or works and the gradual growth in four liberations or gifts. The four austerities concentrate education upon the physical, the vital, the psychic and the mental stages of man. Integral development of physical being, vital being, psychic being and mental being brings about ultimately the transformation of man into a spiritual being. New man, tranformed and spiritualized is the final goal of Aurobindo's theory of education.

There is a stress in primary education on the physical and vital being. Perhaps the vital being is the most important starting point for it consists in a thorough observation of the character to be developed and transformed. It requires, in particular, observation of impulses, energies and desires. Aurobindo called the vital being of man,

> the Life-nature made up of desires, sensations, feelings, passions, energies of action, will of desire, reactions of the desire-soul in man and of all that play of possessive and other related instincts, anger, fear, speed, lust, etc. that belong to this field of nature.[10]

In order that a student understands both the inner world and the world outside of himself, he must observe himself directly and all that happens to himself. To observe what one does and why one does it is the starting point of self-observation. In this way the individual becomes conscious of himself and can begin to exercise control, direction and, finally, mastery over himself. Another aspect of educating the vital being is the utilization of the sense organs. The first work of educationists, according to Aurobindo, is the development and right use of the six senses,

9. *Bulletin of Physical Education*, Vol. III, N. 1 (Feb. 1951), p. 17.
10. *On Yoga*, (1958), Vol. II, Tome I, p. 330.

the training of the senses in accuracy, sensitivity, width and breadth. Development of the senses and an increased physical consciousness give a wider scope and capacity to the individual. In the pragmatic work of teaching, the training of the aesthetic nature of the individual is part of vital education. Aurobindo, like Tagore, would place emphasis on aesthetic training at a very early moment in education; in fact, Aurobindo considered vital education as the training of the aesthetic personality. Such training consists in developing the emotions, human habits and their associations, the rejection of bad habits and the substitution of new ones. With observation and self-knowledge, there comes the need for concentration and, especially, the concentration of vital energies. To concentrate and to gather together one's vital energy is not only necessary but a preliminary step in the growth and self-mastery of character. Thus education of the vital being involves the *tapasya* (discipline) of power, but with an increase in power there comes a liberation from ordinary desires laying the foundation for spiritual life.

Although Sri Aurobindo set forth the broad lines of an educational theory, the Mother enfleshed this outline in *āśram* practice and through substantial writing, especially on physical education. There is a Sanskrit adage that the body is the means to fulfill *dharma* (duty), and Aurobindo understood *dharma* here to mean every ideal which we can propose to ourselves and the realization of them. Physical culture has been from ancient times a part of spiritual development in the Indian traditions. The body has been an opportunity to manifest spirit. In Aurobindo's thought, the body, as all matter, is the creation of the inconscient, and thus man has to open physical life and fill it with power and higher consciousness. The body must be developed, according to Aurobindo, as an "entirely conscious frame and instrument, a conscious sign and seal and power of the spirit."[11] Two conditions in physical education are the awakening of body consciousness and evoking its possibilities as fully as one can. To awaken the body consciousness is to act upon the physical with psychic consciousness. In Aurobindo's words:

11. *Sri Aurobindo and the Mother on Education*, p. 46.

> The physical *sādhana* is to bring down the higher light and power and peace and *ānanda* into the body consciousness, to get rid of the inertia of the physical, the doubts, limitations, eternal tendency of the physical mind, the defective energies of the vital physical nerves and bring in instead the true consciousness there so that the physical may be a perfect instrument af the Divine Will.[12]

He spoke of the divine body, man physically transformed, as a result of the evolution of consciousness, for the transformation that he sought embraced all life, mind and body.

Physical education is completely governed by order, method and discipline. The procedures to be worked out are rigorous, highly detailed and methodical. Yet Aurobindo and the Mother never insisted on a peculiar set of exercises, for their own experiences indicated that no one type of physical *sādhana* need be followed for yogic achievement. Physical education includes multiple goals: control and discipline over physical functions; a harmonious and full development of body and physical movements; the rectification of defects and overcoming physical limitation; and finally, the awakening of body consciousness. The first three goals are achieved through physical exercise, but the last draws upon multiple faculties. The Mother introduced sports in the *āśram* and spoke frequently in support of athletics, gymnastics and games in the school. In ancient India there was a stress on physical growth and the old *āśrams*, before they became monastic, were places where men and boys participated in the full scope of life. There was great controversy in the Aurobindo *āśram* in the beginning over the physical education programmes; many thought that the Mother was making sports and games a physical *sādhana* essential for all. Sports, however, were never obligatory. Although Aurobindo saw no *a priori* reason why sports should not be present, he still considered spiritual disciplines, service, *bhakti* and *yoga* as the essentials. He favoured the *āsanas* (physical exercises) and *prāṇayama* (breathing techniques), the latter which he himself vigorously pursued as a young man, in order to overcome the restlessness of the body and to concentrate

12. *Sri Aurobindo and the Mother on Physical Education*, pp. 48-49.

prāṇic-energy within the body. Education of the physical being is necessary for controlling sexual impulses, and Aurobindo considered sexual mastery necessary for the seeker of truth and a complete eradication of sexuality necessary for the committed ascetic. In some of his later writings, he speculated about the actual transformation of sexuality, its impulses and energies and even organs. Moreover, he supported the emphasis on sports and games in the school because he saw them as a means to renew energy, both physical energy and higher forms of energy. He considered the development of the sporting-spirit contributive toward tolerance, good humour, self-control, consideration of others, friendliness and fair play. Competitive sport, however, had to be done in the right spirit, that is without ambition, and when it was done well it became a means for self-mastery, even the mastery of ego. In the *āśram* school following the period of evening sports, there would be a ten-minute period of concentration in order to recall and spiritualize. Play became an expression of inner consciousness.

The major task in education of the physical is to awaken the aspiration for the divine in the body. The Mother spoke of faith awakening the cells of the body, which was the personal effort of Sri Aurobindo and the Mother in their later years. She urged the continual recalling of past experiences of inner joy and light within the body, and the cultivation of the certitude that the body carries within it its own transformation.[13] The ideal of physical life is beauty, and "You must hold within yourself the living ideal of beauty that is to be recognized," wrote the Mother.[14] Education of the physical being involves the *tapasya* of beauty, and with the growth of beauty there comes a gradual liberation from the conditioning of matter. Physical mastery and spiritual mastery are what Aurobindo's education is fundamentally about. The Mother even believed that India's role was "to teach to the world that matter is false and impotent unless it becomes a manifestation of the spirit."[15]

13. *Ibid.*, pp. 140ff.
14. *Integral Education* p. 47.
15. *Mother India*, Vol. XVII, N. 9 (Oct. 1965), p. iii.

Mental education gathers old knowledge, discovers new knowledge and builds the capacity to use and apply knowledge. It includes cognition, ideas, intelligence and mental perceptions. In the process man becomes the source of knowledge, the knower, the witness and master of his mind. Sri Aurobindo distinguished four classical levels of the mind: *citta*, the storehouse of memory, in which the active memory needs development in selecting and recalling, and the passive memory containing all past experiences, which needs no development; *manas*, the sixth sense, in which all the other senses are gathered as a faculty for development; *buddhi*, the actual instrument of thought disposing and ordering all knowledge, is the most important; and the final level of intuition, inspiration and vision in the extraordinary personality. On the various levels of mind, human effort tries to increase capacity through widening, expansion and complexity of cognition, ideas and perceptions. A major factor in Aurobindo's thought is the continual organization of ideas around a central or higher ideal. In his school, he was never concerned about the teaching of many subjects but urged students to find many approaches to the same subject, that is, many ideas and perceptions that could be organized around some original subject.

Knowledge belongs to a region higher than the mind. "The mind has to be made silent and attentive in order to receive knowledge from above and manifest it," wrote the Mother.[16] There is, consequently, emphasis on mental silence and concentration in the education of the mental being. In training the intellect, the Mother said, "You have to be the Witness watching it reading or writing or talking."[17] An initial step in classical *yoga* is the silence of the mind and with it comes the experience of oneself as witness. With concentration things can be done quickly and with improvement. With mental silence the complete observation of mind takes place for an effective direction and mastery of the mind itself. Education of the mental being involves the *tapasya* of knowledge, and with growth in knowledge there is a gradual liberation from ignorance.

16. *Sri Aurobindo and the Mother on Education*, p. 55.

17. *Mother India*, Vol. XX, N. 10-11 (Dec. 1968), p. 35.

The education of the psychic being is Aurobindo's special contribution to educational theory. In fact, to discover psychic being may be looked upon as the principal function of education for him. The key to an integral personality is the discovery and revitalization of man's psychic centre. Education is a social approach to the growth of personality and the discovery of the psychic centre. Man has the basic psychic need to uncover and to manifest the soul within himself. The necessity for the soul of man to grow in freedom, according to its inner nature, is a fundamental psychic need. For Aurobindo, the psychic being is that centre in man independent of the body and circumstances of life; it is that centre which has universality and limitless expansion in time and space. Psychic being is the psychological centre of the individual. To be conscious of the psychological centre of individual man is the function of education. The psychic being does not observe or watch like the mind, the mental being; instead, it is spontaneous, direct and luminous. The psychic being supports the vital, the physical and the mental being. Through psychic consciousness or presence the individual comes into contact with life and with himself. Evoking the psychic being, in Aurobindo's thought, aims at mastery of the psychic presence in the individual. The difference between psychic experience and spiritual experience is that the former is within the created universe and the latter takes one outside the universe of man. Spiritual education is a return to the unmanifest, beyond time and space; psychic education is higher realization in time and space. "So one can say that the psychic life is the life immortal, endless time, limitless space, ever progressive change, unbroken continuity in the world of forms," wrote Aurobindo.[18] Close touch with one's psychic being leads to ultimate discovery and realization.

In *The Human Cycle*, Sri Aurobindo places the weight of education on the psychic being:

> The true secret whether with child, or man, is to help him find his deeper self, the real psychic entity within. That, if we ever give it a chance to come forward, and still more,

18. *Integral Education*, p. 67.

> if we call it into the foreground as 'the leader of the march set in our front,' will itself take up most of the business of education out of our hands and develop the capacity of the psychological being towards a realization of potentialities.[19]

The objective is to give the psychic being the best opportunity for exercise, expression and growth. Strong will, the personal will to discover the psychic presence is requisite. The starting point is to discover within oneself that which is independent of external reality and the physical body, that is, the discovery of a sense of universality and limitlessness. "Then you decentralize," according to the Mother, "spread out, enlarge yourself; you begin to live in everything and in all beings; the barriers separating individuals from each other break down."[20] Desire, purpose, direction and will are the crucial factors in discovery. "The will for the great discovery should be always there soaring over you . . . ," wrote the Mother.[21] The educative process is twofold. The first step is surrender to that which is beyond ego, and the second step is to will an identification with one's psychic being. In the thought of Sri Aurobindo, the discovery depends upon *yogic* effort: aspiration, rejection of all else, surrender and the divine activity. Education of the psychic being evokes the *tapasya* of love, and with its growth a gradual liberation from suffering.

The four vehicles of learning—the vital, the physical, the mental and the psychic—respectively, cultivate power, beauty, knowledge and love and hence liberate man from material conditioning, desires, ignorance and suffering. This fourfold approach to education is simultaneous, beginning at an early age and all organized homogeneously around the psychic centre. The psychic movement inward which is complemented by opening outward to higher existence brings spiritual transformation. Sri Aurobindo advocated a total spiritual education which gave more importance to the growth of the spirit than intellectual, moral or even religious knowledge. The logic of his theory is the logic of spiritual education; educational

19. *The Human Cycle*, p. 35.
20. *Integral Education*, p. 64.
21. *Ibid.*, p. 66.

praxis is constantly in the realm of spiritual experience. Growth in human consciousness and the complete transformation of human consciousness is the ultimate goal. Aurobindo calls for spiritual education within the world and for the world but not determined by the external world. It is based upon the belief in and the necessity for the spiritual transformation of man. His theory advocates an end to suffering, ignorance, material and psychological needs. It is based upon the possibility of and a conviction about the transformation and transfiguration of the human species.

Supramental education begins with the transformation begun in the discovery of the psychic being. Once transformation takes place education is supramental, from the above downward. To bring into human life supramental power is the further horizon of Sri Aurobindo's educational thought. Supramental education, which was the personal experience of Aurobindo and the Mother, proceeds from above downward and affects not only human consciousness but also the very nature of man and his environment. Aurobindo approached education less from the perspective of existing pedagogy than from the quality of man envisioned in the future. His point of departure was the twenty-first century man. The Mother also had this vision : "We want to show to the world what must be the new man of tomorrow."[22] Education in the evolution of consciousness and in the discovery and development of the psychic being is the prelude to a new man and a new age.

Sri Aurobindo does not have a new system of education for teachers and educators as much as a new attitude towards students.[23] For the student it is a way of living, growing and progressing. In *A System of National Education*, written as early as 1910, Aurobindo enunciated this new attitude in three basic principles of learning: first, nothing can be taught; secondly, the mind has to be continually consulted; and thirdly, work from

22. *Sri Aurobindo Mandir Annual*, N. 3 (Aug. 1964), p. 276.

23. See Pavitra (P.B. Saint-Hilaire) *Education and the Aim of Human Life* (Pondicherry: Sri Aurobindo International Centre of Education, 1967), p. 41. Also helpful as a secondary source is Satprem, *Sri Aurobindo, The Adventure of Consciousness*; also Robert Bainbridge, "Evolution, Education and the Destiny of Man," unpubl. Ph.D. diss., California Institute of Asian Studies, 1971.

the near to the far.[24] These general but normative principles reflect the comprehensiveness and flexibility of his *yoga*. Whatever applies to his method of integral *yoga* applies now to his educational methodology. Aurobindo's *yoga* is not fixed and rigid but acts freely and widely whereby the process accepts all that man is with the understanding that the total man undergoes change. In his *yoga*, the divine power in man gathers all human life into the *yogic* process. Perceiving the vastness and complexity of the process, he believed that one never applies a method well unless it is discovered by oneself. There is a unity and balance between meditation and action, between the silent mind and practical learning. Just as in integral *yoga* there is a correlation between the ascending and descending movements of consciousness, so too in the learning process there is a correlation between the exteriorization and interiorization of knowledge. According to Aurobindo, there must be "the powerful, redemptive retroaction to every advance in insight, illumination, or love."[25] The retroactive movement is the thrust toward synthesis and integral learnmg.

Man is a transitional being for Aurobindo, and in education synthesis is transitional until the individual realizes his psychic being. "All must be transitional until a first, though not a final, true harmonization is achieved by finding our real centre," he said.[26] In speaking of the education of the mind, he distinguished the intellectual faculties and functions of the right hand from those of the left hand. Science, criticism and observation depend upon faculties which function analytically, comparatively and rationally; this is the left hand of the intellect. But art, poetry, music and literature, depend upon those faculties which function comprehensively, creatively and synthetically; these are the faculties and functions of the right hand of the intellect. Man's intellect has a synthetic and integrative role. This is not the final synthesis that education seeks. Through psychic awareness a whole new synthetic capacity is achieved, a capacity which education also seeks. Just as

24. *Integral Education*, pp. 5-6.

25. *Life Divine*, pp. 636-637, quoted in Chaudhuri and Spiegelberg, *The Integral Philosophy of Sri Aurobindo*, p. 131.

26. *Integral Education*, p. 28.

psychic awareness is achieved through the combined effort of mind, heart and will, so too psychic integration is the combined effort of the total man. In education as in integral *yoga*, a global synthesis is sought.

Integration is a vital operation in education since it is the instrument for achieving integral selfhood. As early as 1912 and long before she came to the *āśram* at Pondicherry, the Mother had called for a synthesis of inner development with external activity.[27] In the *āśram* school she recommended that each student set apart time each day to review one's thoughts and to bring order into one's synthesis. She asked the students to organize all their ideas and perceptions around one great central idea which was encompassing. Every thought should be placed before the central idea. If it finds a right relationship, it will be admitted to the broader synthesis, and if it cannot be related to the central idea, it will be rejected.[28] Synthesis in the learning process is an attempt to establish multiple relationships with what is known and to place these relationships against their ultimate relational unity. In mental development everything is considered from many points of view until a thesis and antithesis are formed, and "then by careful reflection the problem must be widened or transcended so that a synthesis is found which unites the two contraries in a larger, higher and more comprehensive idea."[29] A synthetic organization of learning brings about a progressive and broad unification of all knowledge. The purpose of study and activity is "to organize your cerebral capacity," "crystallizing your thought," arriving at knowledge that is "exact and organized."[30] The great synthesis is the work of the divine, for the transformative experience of integral *yoga* is the descent of divine power (*śakti*) as peace in the mind, heart and body of man, and this harmonizes with man's ascending aspiration and surrender to establish a new synthesis. Aurobindo's methodology aims at raising the personality of man qualitatively through synthesis.

27. See The Mother, *Conversations* (Pondicherry: Sri Aurobindo Ashram, 1966) p. 1.
28. *Integral Education*, pp. 55ff.
29. *Sri Aurobindo and the Mother on Education*, p. 55.
30. *Education, Learning* p. 6.

Aurobindo believed that the best order in education is founded on the greatest liberty, "for liberty is at once the condition of vigorous variation and the condition for self-finding."[31] The child must grow freely as an organic person. Every child is a self-developing being, and the role of both parent and educator is to advance self-development. Free progress contributes to the new attitude Sri Aurobindo introduced into the educational method. According to Pavitra, an educationist at the Pondicherry *āśram*, Aurobindo's contribution to education was not only to make the soul the specific object of education but also to hand over the responsibility of education to the student as a means to evoke the soul.[32] The psychic being is evoked by the individual himself, and he must freely find and determine the means to the discovery. Transferring this attitude to education gave birth to the Free Progress System in the Aurobindo *āśram* and its school.

Free progress in the school means that the student proceeds at his own pace. The students choose their subjects of study, cultivate areas of interest and elect to take examinations or not. Aurobindo believed that only one or two subjects should be taken at one time, for study should not proceed by snippets from multiple subjects. He did not think lectures were essential and recommended that they be kept at a minimum. Emphasis in the Aurobindo school is placed upon work sheets, a set of instructions covering the study a student does himself, with the constant availability of the teacher. The Free Progress System naturally limits class size to four or five students. The school does not prepare the student for official examinations, scholarly competition, diplomas or titles. This demonstrates that the goals are not to prepare students to earn money or to build careers. "We study to learn, to know, to understand the world and for the joy that it gives," wrote the Mother.[33] Tests, if requested, are individually adopted for each student and are only meant for the student to check his own progress. To know student progress requires on the part of the teacher intimate

31. Sri Aurobindo, *The Ideal of Human Unity*, abrid. Sisirkumar Ghose (Calcutta: Sri Aurobindo Pathamandir, 1972), p. 98.

32. Pavitra, *Education and the Aim of Human Life*, p. 153.

33. *Education, Learning*, p. 26.

contact and a good psychological knowledge of the student. The Free Progress System can begin with ease at the age of ten if the vital and the physical being have been developed at an earlier age. Without the development of the vital being, the system cannot succeed.

The Mother believed that a child at fourteen should know whether he wanted to study or not, and from this age onward he should have the freedom to develop his own education and to be advised only if asked. But once a student had set his course and selected a plan of study, it was necessary to follow it "honestly, with discipline, regularity and method."[34] The new method, however, was not imposed upon the teachers in the *āśram* school or in the Sri Aurobindo International Centre of Education. Multiple methods were employed, including free progress and Montessori, but no one method was strictly adhered to. Some of the teachers did not adopt the system to their methodology. Free progress, nonetheless, advances both a new attitude to the student and to education as a whole. Open classes, freely selected by the student, advance the principle of freedom and choice in education. Perpetual choice prompts the individual to discover knowledge within himself and to discover his own centre. Free progress implies that education is merely an invitation to learning and is at the most suggestive.

Integral education not only accepts the general goals articulated by Sri Aurobindo but also takes into account the vast complexity of man. A youth educates himself to the degree that he comes to a greater understanding of himself and his universe. Students should be challenged to work for personal and collective transformation. To place before the student the ideal and the challenge of transformation is the work and role of the teacher. In *The Brain of India* Aurobindo, speaking of national education, said : "This conception of the knowing faculty made the removal of *tamas*, the discipling of *rajas* and the awakening of *sattva* the main problem of the teacher. He had to train the student to be receptive of illumination from within."[35] Aurobindo considered the removal of the lethargic tendencies (*tamas*)

34. *Ibid.*, p. 21.

35. Sri Aurobindo, *The Brain of India* (Pondicherry : Sri Aurobindo Ashram, 1967), pp. 17-18.

of the Indian student the initial problem for the teacher, which are eradicated by the challenge for transformation and by continually placing the ideal before the student. The transformation of lethargic proclivities is overcome by sustained interest. The teacher must first interest the child in life, work and knowledge. He awakens the child, without kneading or pressurising him more than he instructs him. The first rule of moral education, for Aurobindo and the Mother, was to invite the student to transformation and learning and not to impose the educative process on him.

Education in this context is not to impart knowledge but to show others how to learn by themselves. Aurobindo rejected the lecture method because it frequently imparts just information. "He (the teacher) does not impart knowledge to him (the student), he shows him how to acquire knowledge," counselled Aurobindo.[36] Since the fundamental task of the teacher is to bring students to know themselves, the teacher basically creates the environment for self-discovery and remains present and available to the student. He informs the environment with things of interest which stimulate mind, emotions and body. The environment, moreover, must be well-organized wherein the adoption of new methods comes with case. Since the initial task of education is to teach the student to concentrate, an environment conducive to quiet and order is necessary. The teacher organizes the students in order that they are led to responsibility and the discovery of inner guidance. An atmosphere of good will and good order helps to induce the psychic opening in the student. Aurobindo believed that it was never too soon to begin psychic education. The second role of the teacher, following upon the creation of an environment, is to be present and available to the needs of the student. In this role, the teacher begins to exert inflence through his own example. Sri Aurobindo spoke of the student-teacher relationship:

> This is a kind of good company, *satsanga*, which can seldom fail to have effect so long as sententious sermonizing is

36. Sri Aurobindo, quoted in Pavitra, *Education and the Aim of Human Life*, p. 110.

> avoided, and becomes of the highest effect if the personal life of the teacher is itself moulded by the great things he places before his pupils.[37]

The life and example of the teacher are communicated, according to Aurobindo, not through verbal communication but through the living enthusiasm, the non-verbal communication of the teacher.[38] Education becomes most effective through example.

The Mother called teaching a sacred trust: "Education is a sacerdocy, teaching is a sacerdocy, and to be at the head of a State is a sacerdocy."[39] This implied the high level of personality expected of the teacher. The personality traits of the teacher consisted, for the Mother, in complete self-control, a sense of the relativity of his importance, the absence of superiority, and a sense that all are equal spiritually.[40] The ideal teacher is beyond egoism, one who has moved beyond intellectuality, one who finds his task and duty an ease. Manoj Dasgupta, a former student and professor of the Sri Aurobindo International Centre of Education, recalled that the most striking feature of his student life in the *āśram* and the Centre was freedom, for the Mother never compelled but merely showed the way.[41] The good teachers, according to the Mother, were those who made inner progress "towards impersonalization, capable of eliminating their egoism, becoming master of their movements, possesing insight, comprehension of others and a patience proof against all test and time."[42] On the other hand, Sri Aurobindo anticipated the quality of *guru* in the teacher:

> He is a man helping his brothers, a child leading children, a Light kindling other lights, an awakened Soul awakening

37. *A Scheme of Education*, p. 39.
38. See Pavitra, *Education and the Aim of Human Life*, p. 111.
39. *Education, Teaching*, p. 10.
40. *Ibid.*, pp. 8-9.
41. Manoj Dasgupta, "Experience of a Student-Professor of the Sri Aurobindo International Centre of Education," *Sri Aurobindo Circle* Twentieth Number, (1964), pp. 46-50.
42. *Mother India*, Vol VIII, N. 4 (Jan. 1959), p. 4.

> other souls, at highest a Power of Presence of the Divine calling to him other powers of the Divine.[43]

Although Aurobindo believed the *guru* was truly the inner self, he pointed to the three instruments of the *guru* as teaching, example and influence. Both he and the Mother spoke of the influence of the *guru* in terms of presence. Commenting on some of the problems and solutions in contemporary India, the Mother wrote:

> Example is more important than instruction, and influence is more important than example. Influence is not the outward authority of the teacher, but the power of his contact, of his presence, of the nearness of his soul to the soul of another, infusing into it, even though in silence, that which he himself is and possesses.

If it is the good company, the *satsanga*, that marks the successful teacher, it is the non-verbal communication through presence that marks the extraordinary teacher, the *guru*. The Mother maintained that "One must be a saint and a hero to be a good teacher, one must become a great *Yogi* to be a good teacher,"[45] because only then could an inner presence, an inner knowledge, love, power and beauty be experienced, communicated and assimilated by the student. The *guru* is a communicator of the gifts of the four great austerities: love, knowledge, power and beauty. These are the achievements of integral education and the results of the development of the integral personality. They are experienced at the feet of and communicated through the presence of the great teacher, the *guru*. The *guru* communicates something of himself, namely, psychic being. Sri Aurobindo spent several decades in silence as did the Mother in the final

43. *On Yoga*, pp. 74-76, quoted in *Sri Aurobindo Mandir Annual*, N. 23 (Aug., 1964), p. 260.

44. The Mother, *On India: Some Problems and Solutions* (Pondicherry: Sri Aurobindo Ashram, 1970), p. 7.

45. *Education, Teaching*, pp. 4-5.

years of her life. Their role of *guru* did not diminish but continued to flourish during these periods. Silent example and influence were a major constituent in the teaching roles of both. They were effective with their disciples because of their capacity to be present with the full integrality of their personalities.

CHAPTER TWELVE

Praxis and Significance

Sri Aurobindo spent thirteen years as a teacher in the Baroda State Service beginning in 1893. He was a part-time lecturer in French and in 1900 was appointed Professor of English. In 1904 he was selected Vice-Principal of Baroda College and also acted as Principal for some months. When his first revolutionary articles appeared in *Indu Prakash* in 1893-94, he castigated the existing education in India and gave hints of an educational reform. National education was one of the key issues in the platform of the Nationalist Party in 1906, but Aurobindo as early as 1893 was calling for resurgence in national education. Although lecturing at Baroda College during these years, he was no extraordinary orator, speaking without gesture or movement but with a stylized prose. In 1906 he moved to Calcutta and became the associate editor of *Bande Mataram*, the Bengali newspaper of the Nationalist Party, and the first Principal of the newly established National College. His educational ideals and their implications started taking concrete form from this time onward. He resigned his leadership of the National College when the government began prosecution against him, and he severed all connections with it during the Alipore trial in 1908. Following his jail experience he founded the *Karmayogin*, an English journal in Calcutta in 1909, and this became the vehicle for his foundational writing on education. He placed education within the context of Indian regeneration to the degree that he called for nationalism within the schools.

In *The Brain of India* (1909), he laid down the *brahmācārya-yoga* axis in education. Relying upon classical notions of Indian education, he viewed *brahmācārya* as the elevation of physical life to levels of spiritual existence and as the strengthening of the spiritual (*satvic*) qualities in man. *The National Value of Art* (1909) followed with his major statement. *A System of National Education* (1910), appearing in *Karmayogin*. He spoke in the former work again of education as the principal means of Indian renewal, and the latter work explicitly revealed his goals, for he spoke in terms of building "sons for the Motherland, to work and to suffer for her. . . . If you will study, study for her sake; train your body and mind and soul for her service."[1] He looked upon India's youth as "children of the past, possessors of the present, creators of the future."[2] The search for the divine in man was raised up as the highest and most specific goal of education: "The chief aim of education should be to help the growing soul to draw out that in itself which is best and make it perfect for a noble use."[3] This first phase of Sri Aurobindo's praxis saw both a concrete involvement in teaching and college administration, and writing, the latter echoing classical Indian thought.

The second phase of Aurobindo's praxis was *āśram* life. He began to draw followers around him during the political activity in Calcutta, and upon leaving for Chandernagore and later for Pondicherry in 1910, a committed nucleus was formed. It was apparent from the beginning that Sri Aurobindo was the teacher. Nolini Kanta Gupta recalls this period:

> Sri Aurobindo had his own novel method of education. It did not proceed by the clock, nor according to a fixed routine or curriculum, that is, there was nothing of the school about it. It went simply and naturally along lines that seemed to do without rules.[4]

1. *Speeches* (1952 edition) quoted in Iyengar, *Sri Aurobindo, A Biography and a History*, Vol. 1, p. 432.
2. *Ibid.*, Vol. 11, p. 632.
3. *Ibid.*, Vol. 1, p. 622.
4. Nolini Kanta Gupta, *Reminiscences*, p. 35.

Aurobindo taught his followers Sanskrit, European languages, literature and philosophy, but most importantly he gradually exposed them to integral *yoga*. In the beginning the Pondicherry community formed a spiritual household where the political exiles lived sparsely, engaged in various activities and became progressively more committed to a full spiritual life. The relationships among the members of the household were relations of emulation, collaboration and brotherhood. It was during the first sixteen years in Pondicherry, the silent years of *yoga*, that Sri Aurobindo edited and wrote for his new journal, *Arya*, which became a major effort of the household. The Mother, then Mira Richard, came in 1920 for permanent residence, and again Aurobindo became the teacher, instructing her in Sanskrit and other Indian languages and philosophy. From his Calcutta days Aurobindo saw the necessity for a new spiritual centre : "It is necessary to create a centre of thought and knowledge which will revolutionize the brain of the nation to as great an extent as its character and outlook have been revolutionized."[5] The Pondicherry community became that new centre of thought. Maintaining that a spiritual search involved an institutional life not separated from the life of society, Aurobindo and his household, although leading a very private life, were never severed from the normal course of life around them. The Sri Aurobindo Āśram, however, did not emerge until 1926 when Aurobindo began a whole new phase in his spiritual journey following the descent of the Overmind.

The *āśram* was organized on a practical basis in 1926 with handing over the direction of the followers and the *āśram* itself to the Mother. Aurobindo has said that "The *Āśram* is the Mother's creation and would not have existed but for her."[6] There had been only four or five companions with Aurobindo until 1922, but the household increased to 25 by 1926. By 1942 under the Mother's direction, the number had jumped to 350 and by 1952 to 800; the increase continued steadily to 1,200 by 1962 and by the 1970s well over 2,000. With the increase in numbers, service departments were formed over the years, for

5. *The Brain of India*, quoted in *A Scheme of Education*, p. 62.

6. Quoted in Narayan Prasad, *Life in Sri Aurobindo Ashram* (Pondicherry: Sri Aurobindo Ashram, 1968), p. 18.

example, kitchen, agriculture, domestic, housing and furniture, construction and even electric service. The work of the *āśram* was an intimate part of the *sādhana*, for the Mother had said: "In works, aspiration towards perfection is true spirituality."[7] Everything in the evolution of the *āśram* received the benefit of the Mother's insight and nothing was done without her knowledge or sanction. The whole growth of the Sri Aurobindo Āśram advanced through her direction. In the later years she gradually withdrew from the visible direction of it, and in the 1960s she began the final years of seclusion and privacy: "I withdrew from all details and kept myself at a distance, sending the right inspiration to each worker in his own field."[8] One disciple remarked that the *āśram* was not a mere institution but an organic growth, an organism, neither planned nor built, a natural and living expression of Sri Aurobindo's personality.[9] The significance of the *āśram*, in Aurobindo's educational work is that it was the testing-ground for his educational theory and the matrix out of which grew a school, a university and a city.

The *āśram* school began in December 1943, for the children of the disciples, with the *āśram* buildings and grounds as classrooms and the disciples as teachers. By the early 1950s, it had over 200 students and more than 50 teachers. The full development of the personality with special emphasis upon the discovery of the psychic being was the specific focus of its education. The Free Progress System was initiated and the teachers, practioneers of integral *yoga*, entered into the creation of the new personality of Sri Aurobindo's vision. With the admittance of children into the *āśram* life came a natural emphasis upon the needs of the young. The austerity of the *āśram* was less visible as programmes in education, especially physical activities, brought new vitality to the general atmosphere. The Mother consistently held before the *āśram* school the high ideal: "If we have a school here, it must be different from the millions of schools in the world; it must give the children a chance to distinguish

7. *Ibid.*, p. 27.
8. *Ibid.*, p. 29.
9. Madhav P. Pandit, in *Handbook*, *Sri Aurobindo University Centre* (Pondicherry: Sri Aurobindo Ashram, 1968), p. 16.

between ordinary life and Divine Life. . . ."[10] A further step in educational praxis came with the death of Aurobindo in 1950.

At a conference called in Pondicherry in April 1951, a resolution was passed to establish the Sri Aurobindo International University Centre. The formal inauguration took place in January 1952, and the first term opened in December 1953. The plan called for education from pre-school through graduate study. The guiding principles were the homogeneity of the scholarly community and the continuity of education from childhood through the adult years. The Centre was conceived as an integral part of the *āśram*, for the *āśram* remained the matrix. The roots of the Centre were to remain especially in the *āsram* school-community, since the school was the nucleus for innovative education and gave direction to the Centre. The Centre was international from its inception. Sri Aurobindo conceived the scheme of the university some years previously "so that the elite of humanity may be made ready who would be able to work for the progressive unification of the race and who at the same time would be prepared to embody the new force descending upon earth to transform it."[11] He envisioned a synthetic organization of all nations each contributing its own genius and striving for unity. They were to be grouped around a wide ideal in order to include all cultures and civilizations. Aurobindo conceived the international dimension of the Centre as a positive unifying element. The Centre was to help the individual become conscious of the genius of his own nation and to put him into immediate contact with modes of thought and living of all people. The "Aims and Objectives" from the 1963 Handbook of the Centre reflect Aurobindo's inspiration:

> To evolve and realize a system of integral education, and to make it a dynamic ideal for society.
> To organize an environment and an atmosphere affording inspiration and facilities for the exercise and development

10. *Bulletin of Physical Education* (Nov. 1963), "Questions and Answers."

11. *Education, General Principles*, p. 25.

> of the essential five aspects of the personality: the physical the vital, the mental, the psychic and the spiritual.
> To emphasize the unity of all knowledge and to bring Humanities and Science close together into a real sense of affinity for the benefit of both.
> To develop the sense of the oneness of mankind and international collaboration.
> To discover and prepare for the role that India has to play in the formation of the new international harmony.[12]

In short there was an attempt from the very beginning to integrate spirituality and education in the progressive realization of integral education. In 1959 the Mother dropped the word university from its title and called it a Centre of Education in order to give it a wider scope.

The Sri Aurobindo International Centre of Education was planned for 1,400 to 1,500 students. Three educational divisions soon emerged, the primary, secondary and higher education. Pre-school involved students for two or three years, primary and secondary education followed a plan of four and six years respectively. Higher education embraced both the arts and sciences but soon evolved into four basic faculties; arts, sciences, engineering and technology, and physical education. Education became year-round with a brief vacation of fifteen to twenty days in November and December. No fees or tuition or academic expenses were asked, just nominal payment for room and board. Since the teachers were *sādhaks* (spiritual seekers), they were not paid. English and French were the medium of instruction in all non-language classes. A detailed and elaborate physical education curriculum was established in 1952 which is followed even today. There was no instruction in the great world religions since the *āśram* did not conceive itself attached to any one religion. The Mother took a leading role in the conception and execution of the Centre and an equally active role in teaching. She taught French to the young in the open air for many years. Classes on Sri Aurobindo were held even for the elementary levels; advanced students would be introduced to *The Life Divine* and *The Synthesis of Yoga*. More

12. See *Handbook, Sri Aurobindo University Centre*, 1953, pp. 10-11.

advanced instruction in yogic knowledge was given only at the postgraduate level for those who practised it and had a capacity for it.

The Mother composed a prayer for the students which became endeared at the Centre:

> Make us the hero warriors we aspire to become. May we fight successfully the great battle of the future that is to be born against the past that seeks to endure: so that the new things may manifest and we be ready to receive them.

She continually placed before students and teachers alike the special attitude and high aspiration of Sri Aurobindo. In speaking to students, she said, "If you wish truly to profit by your study here, try to look at things and understand them with a new eye and a new understanding based on something higher, something deeper, something wider, something more true, something which is not today but will be one day."[13] The Centre was organized around an atmosphere that was relaxed, free, and as one school-boy recalled with "no compulsory word in the whole *āśram* or university."[14] The Free Progress System has been pursued, and although academic levels do exist students can take some courses at one level, other courses at another level. Until 1967 both sequences, Free Progress and traditional, were followed in the Centre. In 1968 an attempt was made to integrate the two sequences. From the beginning many methods were utilized, not only those suggested by Sri Aurobindo and the Mother but also experimental education initiated by Tagore, Dalton and other Western educationists. The student-teacher ratio has been kept small with 900 students and 200 teachers in 1970.

In 1964 educational research was drawn into the Department of Information and Research under the direction of Norman C. Dowsett. Educationists from all over the world visit the Pondicherry programmes today. The Centre was visited in 1965 by an education committee of the Indian government,

13. *Sri Aurobindo and the Mother on Physical Education*, p. 107.

14. Gautam, "A School-Boy Visitors' Impressions of the Ashram," *Mother India* (May 1953), p. 59.

and although supportive of the endeavours of the Centre it had difficulty in accepting "a change in consciousness" as an educational goal, recommending a more social and pragmatic orientation.[15] Nonetheless, the *āśram* and the Centre have continued to study on many levels the evolutionary process and the evolution of consciousness. Kireet M. Joshi, an official of the Centre, still points to the basic research of the Centre as the knowledge and integration of the psychological principles of gnostic being. The Centre remains committed to a synthesis of knowledge and work culture whereby *yoga* is the dynamic principle of education.[16] A national educational seminar held in Pondicherry in 1967 committed itself to humanist education, believing that spirit provides a solution to human problems.[17] Although the Centre seems to have developed elaborate testing schemes, there has been a clear change in the children over the years. One educationist at the Centre for several decades has observed that the children are no longeer in chaos, physically, vitally or psychically, but their thought is integral to feelings, emotions and actions.[18]

In February, 1968, the Mother announced at the celebration of her ninetieth birthday the beginning of Auroville, the latest step in Aurobindian education. Children from 120 countries poured handfuls of dirt into a lotus-shaped urn and signed the Charter of Auroville some five miles north of Pondicherry. Auroville, the City of Dawn, is envisioned as planetary, consciously evolutionary, unitary, electronic, the city of the twenty-first century for the twenty-first century man. The Charter reads :

15. See Indra Sen, "Visit of the Education Commission to Pondicherry," *Mother India*, Vol. XVII, No. 10-11 (Nov.-Dec., 1965), pp. 45-48.
16. See Kireet M. Joshi, "Sri Aurobindo Ashram as an International Institution of Research in Education and Yoga," *The Advent*, Vol. XXIV, No. 2 (April 1967), pp. 23-47.
17. See "Education for One World", *Mother India*, Vol. XX, No. 8 (Sept. 1967), pp 546ff.
18. Norman C. Dowsett, "Change of Climate in the United Nations Organization," *Mother India*, Vol., XXIII, No. 2 (March 1970), pp. 93-94.

> Auroville belongs to nobody in particular. Auroville belongs to humanity as a whole. But to live in Auroville one must be a willing servitor of the Divine Consciouseness. Auroville will be the place of an unending education, of constant progress and a youth that never ages.
> Auroville wants to be the bridge between the past and the future. Taking advantage of all discoveries from without and from within Auroville will boldly spring towards future realizations.
> Auroville will be a site of material and spiritual researches for a living embodiment of an actual Human Unity.

Although still in the planning stage, Auroville has for its goal the search for a new education in a new society. To live in Auroville is conceived of as an education itself. "Auroville is education," as one Aurobindian puts it[19]. The university of Auroville will be identified with the town itself wherein a synthesis of nations, of truth and knowledge, ideologies and cultures, realities past, present and future will be gathered. It will seek a new culture that is universal and integral. Conceived as a university city of fifty thousand, the citizens will be dedicated to the education and evolution of man. Every citizen, every building and institution within the city, will fulfill an educative purpose. The Mother has conceived it as a place of "unending education, of constant progress, and of youth that never ends."[20] Since education is transformative, Auroville wants to provide a learning environment which conditions a different type of person. The environment of the town is planned to both humanize and transform its inhabitants. The city hopes to evoke the educational triad of freedom, exploration andpl ay.

Auroville is the furthest horizon of Sri Aurobindo's thought and the Mother's inspiration. At the moment it has been thoroughly worked out on the drawing board, but it is still a modest beginning. The city will be constructed within a concentric architectural design consisting of four zones, cultural,

19. See "Auroville and Education," *Mother India*, Vol. XXII, No. 6 (July 1970), p. 353.
20. *Ibid.*

industrial, residential and educational, representing the four essential activities of man. The zones surround the centre, the Matrimandir—the soul of Auroville—a golden sphere emerging out of the earth, surrounded by gardens, a place for meditation and aspiration. The Matrimandir is now in process of construction. Receiving support from a variety of individuals from many countries and from the government of India and UNESCO, life has already begun in Auroville. Several small communities have been formed and the building of the city is slowly moving forward with several hundred residents.

Yvonne Artard has been given the task by the Mother to direct education, and this has become the special work of the Aspiration Community. Eucation begins here with the education of the mother, for the society is to be dedicated to the service of the young. In Auroville no child will be obliged to live with his family, for he may choose a second or third family since the educational unit is the whole of society. When asked to name the building which would serve as the first school in Auroville, the Mother said it shall be called the Last School. In order to show the unicity of the concept and the life anticipated, the first journal of Auroville, an educational review, was called *Equals One*=1. The journal is attempting to research and to advance the educational direction set by Sri Aurobindo. Goals have been set so that the entire conception and execution of Auroville is educational; first, education will embrace the entire town, everything will have an educative role; secondly, a bank of knowledge, a centre of information will exist; thirdly, education will be especially centered in Aurodevenir, a recreational and educational park with gardens, pavillions and play areas; fourthly, a centre of learning for future mothers and children of less than four will exist in order to begin education at the earliest possible age; a youth centre will exist wherein youth could do voluntary service, leading a monastic and austere life; and finally, help to village children will be given whereby every Tamil villager will receive a proper diet and each Auroville adult will adopt at least spiritually one Tamil child.

To bring to realization such enterprises as Auroville, the Sri Aurobindo International Centre of Education and the *āśram* itself, Aurobindo drew upon the peculiar cast of the

Indian heritage, namely, its psychological tradition. The aims of the *āśram*, the Centre and Auroville are the same: to experiment with the evolution of consciousness and its powers. The praxis, Aurobindo's Action as it is called by the *sādhaks*, distinctively reflects the personality of Aurobindo himself, for integral *yoga* is a synthesis of all psychic principles and powers, of knowledge and work. The Mother proclaimed in the educational venture:

> We are attending on the birth of a new world, not yet recognized, not yet felt, denied by most; but it is there, endeavouring to grow and quite sure of the result. The road to reach is a new road that has never before been traced; none went by that, none did that. It is a beginning, a universal beginning. . . .[21]

The whole pattern of Aurobindo, Mahatma Gandhi and Rabindranath Tagore as educationists points to a community of outlook. They have been extraordinary experimentors in areas of the mind, socio-political life, and the world of language and literature. They were primarily experimenters in education because they were basically teachers. The three represented a conscious continuity with the past Indian culture and religious heritage, and at the same time they possessed the aspiration and vision for the future of India and, in fact, the world community. They drew their strength from their country whose spiritual potentiality existed in its children. By going to the children, the youth, the most educable, their theory and praxis have continued beyond them.

21. "The Ashram," *Mother India*, Vol. XX, No. 10-11 (Nov.—Dec. 1968) p. 6.

PART FOUR

CONCLUSION:

RELIGIOUS PERSONALITY AND EDUCATION

CHAPTER THIRTEEN

The Religious Personality as Teacher

It is not unusual for a religious personality in India to develop an educational theory and a particularized system of education. Swami Vivekananda was the first at the end of the last century to call for and to initiate practical renewal in Indian education. Acarya Vinoba, Gandhi's successor, also devoted much effort to the problem of national education. Contemporary ascetics continue to develop highly personalized *yogas*. Swami Vivekananda's educational thought can be summed up in the term "man-making" for he was primarily concerned with the building of character, a goal similarly accepted by Mahatma Gandhi.[1] From their own perspective Vivekananda, Gandhi, Tagore and Sri Aurobindo were concerned with total education, the full development of man. Their educational thought and their systems were imbued with their life-philosophies. And man was their supreme consideration.

1. Sisir Kumar Ghose, "Total Education," *Mother India*, Vol, XVIII, No. 7 (August 1966), p. 98. For the Educational theory of Swami Vivekananda see: Sri T.S. Avinashlingam, *Educational Philosophy of Swami Vivekananda* (Coimbatore: Sri Ramakrishna Vidyalaya, 1964); T.S. Avinashilingam, comp., *Education—Swami Vivekananda* (Coimbatore: Sri Ramakrishna Vidyalaya, 1958); T.S. Avinashilingam and K. Swaminathan, *World Teachers on Education* (Coimbatore: Sri Ramakrishana Vidyalaya, 1958).

A prevailing humanism provided the focus of the life-philosophies and the educational thought of the three figures under study here. They were concerned with the total education of the person, because their life-philosophies were substantially humanistic. Just as their life-philosophies were differentiated by their own perspectives, so too their educational humanism was personalized. Gandhi's humanism was thoroughly activistic and operational whereby man was best understood and best educated through activity.[2] It reflected his basic life-philosophy, that is, *karma-yoga*. Rabindranath Tagore, on the other hand, possessed a creative humanism whereby man consciously entered into community with his fellow man, nature and the greater universe. Again this reflected Tagore's life-philosophy, that is, *ānanda-yoga*. Sri Aurobindo, also concerned with the total education of man, enunciated a transcendental humanism whereby man was perfected through the mind and growth in human psychology. His life-philosophy of *pūrṇa-yoga* (integral) involved full human development through the psychic being. Hence humanity was the regulative image in their educational thought and praxis because it was their basic philosophical stance. Each sought to make his educational system a vehicle for a distinctive philosophy of life whether it was *karma-yoga*, *ānanda-yoga* or integral *yoga*.

Their attitude toward education was determined by their conception of human nature and the future of man. Clear differences, however, existed, among them. Gandhi's educational goals were quite specific and concrete while Tagore's were more universal and plastic. Gandhian education in terms of aims and objectives could be included within Tagore's broader outlook. Sri Aurobindo embraced the largest possible perspective for the present and future evolution of man, and both the Gandhian and Tagorean goals could be included within his scope. They agreed that education was the special work of man. While Gandhi saw the role of education in terms of social and economic development, Tagore viewed it in more liberal and artistic terms. Sri Aurobindo, who placed

2. See Reena Mookerjee, "Gandhi and Tagore: On Man," *Gandhi Centenary Volume* (Santiniketan: Visva-Bharati University, 1969), p. 159.

emphasis upon *karma-yoga* within his *āśram*, was still more comprehensive by stressing every dimension of work from the physical to the mental and finally to the spiritual. Gandhi would consider both Tagore and Sri Aurobindo as too general and abstract in their conceptions of man and the direction of education. Tagore, on the other hand, could possibly agree with Sri Aurobindo on his basic vision of man, but Tagore could not include Aurobindo's gnostic being within the limits of his scope. Gandhi was more utilitarian in his approach to education and the future of man; yet Tagore was more open to risks both in educational theory and praxis than either Gandhi or Sri Aurobindo. Tagore had a clearer appreciation of the differences between the useful and the beautiful, both of which he believed must enter into the educative process and the growth of man.[3] Sri Aurobindo, however, had a better grasp of initiating education and human development at that point where an individual was in the course of his personal growth, and his comprehensive plan assimilated individuals no matter how little or how greatly they had already entered into human development. Gandhi and Tagore, however, were more successful in projecting both an image of man and an educational philosophy that directly concerned the masses and national life.

Since their educational thought was imbued with their life-philosophies, Tagore, Gandhi and Sri Aurobindo established a pattern of living for the teacher and the taught alike. The aims of good education in the past Indian experience were always one with the aims of life. In ancient times education distinguished between the knowledge of things and the knowledge of the self. Integral education existed when both were achieved, and educational decay resulted when one or the other, the knowledge of things or the knowledge of the self, was lost. Gandhi, Tagore and Sri Aurobindo highlighted this perception in their systems and attempted to embrace both. Their educational ideals were linked to the ultimate value of things. Swami Vivekananda recognized this at the turn of the century when he observed

3. See K.G. Saiyidain, *The Humanist Tradition in Indian Educational Thought* (London: Asia Publishing House, 1966), p. 52.

that education must "solve the problems of life and this is what is engaging the profound thoughts of the modern world, but which was solved in our country thousands of years ago."[4] Although Tagore, Gandhi and Sri Aurobindo perceived the ultimate value of things in a truly Indian sense, they were basically unorthodox Hindus. Nonetheless, they achieved continuity with the past and with the cultural development of India. Once reason for continuity with the past, at least in their educational theory and praxis, was the strong tendency toward interiorization of the educational process. The interiorization of the process was present because they saw the necessity to achieve in education both an empirical knowledge and a knowledge of the self. Even in establishing continuity with the cultural development of India, they saw the interior development of culture as the point of continuity between the past and the present.

The whole pattern of Indian education in the last century, the pattern of world education for that matter, was to imitate the best of European liberal education. A great dissatisfaction arose as a response to this. To meet this dissatisfaction Indian educators, especially Vivekananda, Gandhi, Tagore and Vinoba, persistently experimented in education. As they grasped the necessity to experiment with new aims and new forms in education, they deeply involved themselves in teaching. Gandhi was always the teacher, intrinsically the teacher, educating either himself or others. Tagore's major public activity in life was education; Sri Aurobindo began public service as a professional teacher and spent the last forty years of his life personally instructing his disciples. In their teaching the particularity of their thought emerged. For Tagore the teacher must increase the sensitivity of the student, while for Gandhi the development of moral will and strength were the teacher's objective. Sri Aurobindo saw the teacher as part of the environment which elicited psychic awareness. Vinoba and Swami Vivekananda also brought something special to their teaching, namely, the cultural growth of the student and

4. Swami Vivekananda, quoted in Sisir Kumar Ghose, "Ideals of Indian Education", *Sri Aurobindo Circle, Nineteenth Number* (1963), p. 84.

social effort, respectively. Even with these specific differences all shared a communality because they sought total education for the future of man. Their life-philosophies, drawing upon the Indian tradition and contiguous with it, brought man to an interiorization of the total educative process. Knowledge of the self could be gained along with the knowledge of things. They shared a communality at the most significant levels: namely, education and religion touched in the process of human growth and change. Tagore, Gandhi and Sri Aurobindo looked to education as that place wherein man was transformed. And transformation is always the work of religion.

Their life-philosophies influenced their education and thought because their personalities shaped their life-philosophies. Rabindranath Tagore was an *ānanda-yogin*; this was the focus of his whole personality. *Ānanda-yoga* was also the most distinctive aspect of his philosophy and his educational theory and praxis. Mahatma Gandhi was a *karma-yogin*, and this was the basic quality of his personality. *Karma-yoga* was the most contributive facet of his philosophy and his educational thought and pedagogy. Sri Aurobindo was the supreme integral *yogin*. Integral *yoga* was the essential quality of his philosophical synthesis, his educational thought and praxis. The religious personality of these three figures formed everything they were to say or do concerning any aspect of life.

Since they were extraordinary personalities, education and religion touched in their educational systems, in their experimentation and in their role as teachers. Although their schools did not overtly teach the great religions, religion and education came together naturally in their institutions. This was due to the broad religious idealism upon which the systems were founded and to the personalities of the founders themselves. In their own time, Gandhi and Sri Aurobindo, though much less Tagore, were recognized both publicly and by their intimates as outstanding religious personalities. They assimilated religion and education in such a way that the religious dimension became apparent in their educational systems. In their experimentation, Gandhi, Tagore and Sri Aurobindo focused upon the social, the aesthetic and the mental potentialities of their students. Gandhi's experimentation resulted in a religion of service; Tagore's experimentation resulted in a religion of humanity; and Sri Aurobindo's experimentation effected a religion of gnostic being. In all cases religion and education were confronted in educational experimentation. Finally, as they became more visible in their role as teachers, education and religion became more indistinguishable. Gandhi and Sri Aurobindo were religious educators, religious teachers; because of the fundamental humanism of Rabindranath Tagore, it may be less obvious that he was a religious educator. They confronted education and religion in a subtle and unobtrusive manner, whereby the confrontation was implict in all that they said or did as teachers. They established further continuity with India's past for the extraordinary teacher was the *guru,* the religious educator.

Human development in India has always moved simultaneously on two levels, the empirical and the transcendental. Just as education sought empirical knowledge along with knowledge of the self, so too the good teacher instructed on both the empirical and transcendental levels at one and the same time. The *guru* instructs on the transcendental level because human liberation (*mokṣa*) is part of and within the process of human development. Hence the religious quest is inherent in the human quest. The three traditional vehicles for human perfection are the scriptures (*śāstra*), inner zeal and the teacher (*guru*). At a point of higher development in the spiritual quest, the three vehicles are interiorized to the degree that the supreme scripture is discovered in the heart and the individual resonates with it, that inner zeal becomes the overwhelming aspiration of the heart, and that the supreme *guru* is the *guru* within the seeker. Until this moment of higher development arrives, though, man must rely upon the direction and insight from the written scripture, the vocal prayers and visible acts of worship, and the living *guru*. India has had a great concern for the living holy man, the person of higher wisdom, the *guru*, and this is true today as much as it was in past centuries. He is frequently the one who imparts the wisdom of the scriptures and inspires the individual toward liberation.

Because of the long development of the concept of the teacher and the vast range and variety of his mission and style, it is difficult to uncover any simple structure for the personality or the meaning of *guru*.[5] *Guru* is used in the sense of teacher in the *Chāndogya Upaniṣad* but even at this early moment in history other terms were employed. One who imparted only the sacred Vedas was a teacher (*upādhyāya*); one who imparted any socio-religious knowledge was also a teacher (*ācārya*); one who performed priestly functions as healer, exorcist, diviner, seer, prophet or bard was equally a teacher (*purohita*). The *Law of Manu* gave to the *guru* three specific functions: namely, to perform sacraments (*saṃkāras*) to maintain the student in learning and to impart the Vedas. However, not every wandering ascetic or holy man was teacher. What distinguished the *guru* from the ordinary *ṛṣi* or *sādhu* (holy man or ascetic) was a particular type of leadership, a fatherhood. The notion of *guru* as father was pan-Indian. He was to lead one from birth to immortality. A student would forsake his family and become a son of the *guru*. In the classical *upanayana* ceremony, the rite of initiation for the twice-born, the youth became a son of the teacher and took on the burden of the teacher's needs and entered into a typical father-son relationship. The *guru* was a spiritual preceptor and his superiority rested on the conviction of the community that his knowledge and teaching were both powerful and of a transcendent origin. The spirituality and the discipline (*yoga*) of the *guru* were believed to be efficacious because just as the teacher was liberated so too could he lead others to liberation. In the course of Indian history, the term lost a great deal of its precision and meaning. At the present time a *guru* in the broadest sense is a type of mediator. He is a mediator of the sacred, of great power and knowledge, and at the same time a saintly and ascetic personality.

Sri Aurobindo fulfilled the most classical notion of *guru* for both disciples and those who knew of him; Mahatma Gandhi in the affections of the masses was more the living saint but a *guru* certainly to his intimates; Rabindranath Tagore was not esteemed as *guru* during his lifetime although he was called Gurudev by Gandhi. Sri Aurobindo had taken upon himself

5. A Study of the historical development of *guru* can be found in Jan Gonda, *Change and Continuity in Indian Religions* (The Hague: Mouton, 1965).

the role of *guru* as early as 1911 for he wrote at that time:"... I am now able to put myself into men and change them, removing darkness and bringing light, giving them a new heart and a new mind."[6] Not only his direction and teaching but also his *darśan* (sight of the *guru*) and the touch of the *guru* had transformative effect upon his disciples and others. In similar manner Gandhi's intimate followers were changed in mind and heart by him, and the masses constantly sought his *darśan*. No such phenomena has been recorded in the life of Rabindranath Tagore other than the awe inspired by his presence during his tours in Europe and America.

Perhaps a more flexible term, one that would embrace all three, is the Hindu notion of saint (*sant*). The Indian *sant* must be a living figure, unlike the Western saint, in order to be efficacious. He is the model who stimulates and encourages others toward liberation. The *sant* more than an object of veneration is a symbol of an ideal, an experience and a knowledge elevates him above the ordinary individual. His essential quality is true understanding, that is, he has a discrimination of the whole universe, of what is peripheral from what is lasting.[7] Power reveals itself in the *sant* since he possesses something timeless and unchanging. Power emanates from him and is manifested by him in wisdom, presence or physical signs. While both Mahatma Gandhi and Sri Aurobindo were universally acclaimed as saints during their lives, the personality of *sant* could also be attributed to Rabindranath Tagore.

Indian *sants* have been called "epistemological saints" because with them true understanding and new wisdom is inserted into the whole universe.[8] They are epistemological personalities because they communicate new ways of knowing and bring about new consciousness. The epistemological *sant* achieves an identity between the knower and the knowledge. History confirms Mahatma Gandhi as one with *ahiṃsā*, and Rabindranath Tagore as one with aesthetic feeling and the

6. Sri Aurobindo, quoted in K.R. Srinivasa Iyengar, *Sri Aurobindo, A Biography and a History* p. 1035.
7. See Betty Heimann, *Facets of Indian Thought* (London: George Allen & Unwin, Ltd., 1964), pp. 78-80. I am indebted to Heimann's work for many of my perceptions on the Indian *sant*.
8. *Ibid.*, p. 79.

enternal *ānanda*, and Sri Aurobindo as one with psychic awareness and gnostic being. An extraordinary teacher is one whose teaching is incarnated in himself and systematically incarnated in others. The teacher who possesses this epistemological possibility in Hinduism imparts knowledge not only by teaching but also by example and grace. Teaching by example brings about a type of self-discovery, and Tagore, Gandhi and Sri Aurobindo utilized this more indirect method. More specifically they influenced those close to them by their grace (*dīkṣā*), that is, by an intimate experience of their own identity with knowledge. This is evidenced in the lives of Sri Aurobindo and Mahatma Gandhi. Their actual teaching by word or action or silence, whether within a learning context or not, was another means of instruction used by them.

The *guru-sant* possessed a special presence, a presence filled with life. In its oldest usage, in the *Ṛgveda*, *guru* signified that which was weighty and mighty. The Sanskrit word *guru* and the Latin *gravitas* (heavy, weighty) are etymologically related. A *mantra* in ancient times could be weighty; a prayer, a song, a sacred duty could be weighty. When *guru* came to connote one who because of special knowledge had conspicuous power, it conveyed the notion of mighty knowledge, mighty power. The *guru* was a weighty and mighty personality. His presence and his knowledge and his personality were felt. In both the East and the West one can experience the power of the saint or preceptor, which universally means to experience the weight of his knowledge, the weight of his personality and presence. The *guru* has an ontological presence. One experiences before him the weight and power of being. To speak of the ontological presence of the *guru-sant* is to describe theoretically the experienced presence of sacral being within the teacher. The high religious personality, moreover, is not necessarily distinct, at least in the sequence of time, from the experienced presence of sacral being. Professor Philip Ashby speaks of the saint in this manner:

> The holy person, in essence, is not something distinct from the Ultimate Wisdom he or she possesses. The person is merely the present physical embodiment, incarnation, of the Ultimate Wisdom Itself. He or she is the means to

> Ultimate Knowledge which is identical with Ultimate Being, and at the same time is Ultimate Knowledge or Being. Speaking theologically, the epistemological means and the ontological end are ultimately one and the same.[9]

To speak of the extraordinary teacher as an ontological presence is to have experienced the weight of his personality to such a degree that knower and knowledge are one, that knowledge and being are one, that meaning and existence are one within him. This is not merely the experience of the teacher-saint in the Indian tradition alone but has considerable universality. It expresses the experiences of the disciples of Sri Aurobindo as well as Mahatma Gandhi and the many ordinary men and women who sought the *darśan* of both. There is a little recorded evidence of similar experiences in the life of Rabindranath Tagore also.

The personalities of Tagore, Gandhi and Sri Aurobindo far surpassed their educational systems. Their impact as teachers was due neither to the particular methodology employed in their schools and *āśrams* nor to their educational ideals. They were extraordinary teachers because of the impact of their personalities. They were weighty personalities, personalities who embodied a moment of *kairos*, an opportune moment wherein something was said not only of significance concerning man and his cosmos but also a restoration of man and cosmos was taking place within them and around them. Rabindranath Tagore's singular insight into the educational process was that education resulted from the interaction of one personality upon another.[10] He further believed that only through the medium of personality could truth be communicated.[11] This is true of the *guru-sant*. The vital energy of the *guru* is transferred to the disciple by the former's personality. Whether one encounters the example, the presence, the sight or touch of the *guru*, vitality is communicated to the disciple through

9. Philip H. Ashby, *Modern Trends in Hinduism* (New York: Columbia University Press, 1974), p. 78.
10. See Rinibas Bhattacharya, *Tagore and the World* (Culcutta: Dasgupta and Co., 1961), p. 106.
11. Rabindranath Tagore, *Letters from Abroad* (Madras: S. Ganesan, 1924), p. 13.

the teacher. Sri Aurobindo observed that "The greatest Master is much less a Teacher than a Presence pouring the divine consciousness and its constituting light and power and purity and bliss into all who are receptive around him."[12] The personality of the master becomes the medium for new life. Although verbal teaching may enlarge the capacity of the disciple and remove defects and limitations in the pursuit of it, the personality of the master is the major source of new life for the disciple. When a powerful personality encounters a less developed personality, the former can achieve a psychic opening in the latter whereby new understanding and insight are gained. When a saintly personality, a divine personality, is experienced, the opportunity for psychic communion exists and through communion of the two personalities the possibility of spiritual renovation is enhanced. Thus the *guru* fashions a new personality through the power and psychic achievements of his own personality.

The transference of consciousness, moreover, take place through the medium of the *guru's* personality. Consciousness in this case is the relational vitality heightening man's spiritual, mental, affective and physical life. Personality communicates consciousness from one to the other and is the means by which the *guru* shares vitality with a disciple. For Tagore knowledge is to know the relationships of things and personality expresses this knowledge. Consciousness or relational awareness, for him, is communicated through the personality. Gandhi devoted his life toward raising the consciousness of the Indian people keeping in view not only national liberation but also personal liberation, and it was effected by raising the relationships between individuals, between an individual and his country and between an individual and society. To the degree that Gandhi's personality was communicative, to that degree he was able to transform relationships and change the consciousness of the people or an opponent in a protest situation. Sri Aurobindo looked upon Consciousness-Force as the relational quality of the godhead which could be shared with mankind through the medium of Supermind. Supermind is the divine personality, the medium for the transference and

12. Sri Aurobindo, quoted in Iyengar, *Sri Aurobindo*, Vol. II, p. 1027.

transformation of consciousness. In short, a new personality is attained through the impact of another personality which can communicate a higher consciousness. This is the function of the teacher. The potency of the living *guru* imparts consciousness through his personality. When an epistemological personality is present, that is, when there is no differentiation between knower and knowledge, a new consciousness is created. Likewise, when the *guru* possesses an ontological presence, that is, when there is no dichotomy between being and knowledge, a new consciousness is created.

The most subtle area for observation is the relationship between *guru* and disciple. A profound interaction takes place in the relationship as the vital energy of the teacher is projected into it. Consciousness by means of the relational vitality of the teacher is dynamically inserted into the relationship. In the educative process which in most cases advances progressively, the relationship is raised and intensified as greater relational life, in terms of energy and consciousness, enters into the relationship. But it is the weight of the personality of the teacher which alone can project and insert new life into the teacher-student relationship.

There is an Indian axiom that kings are respected only in their own country, but the teacher is respected everywhere. Respect for the teacher is typical in Indian education, and respect for the *guru*, which is a type of devotion to him, is necessary if the work of education is to be successful. If education is a drawing forth of the inner man to the threshold of his own possibilities, a quality of faith in the teacher is requisite. Indian education in its best expression has been the drawing forth of the individual, the whole man, toward the fulfilment of his own being. The challenge to the teacher and his consequent obligation are obvious. Faith in the teacher is necessary if he is to bring about new awareness, and a communion of consciousness

The role of the *guru-sant* implies that he not only leads one to perfection, but he is also the *locus*, the context for perfection. The extraordinary teacher in this tradition is not merely an extraodinary person. He is in fact suprapersonal because he is basically the context for the divine activity to be carried out. He is the most important aspect of the environment for spiritual development. Professor Betty Heimann has likened the Indian *sant* to "suprapersonal stepping-stones to perfection."[13] What justifies and necessitates education in Indian life is liberation (*mokṣa*) in time and history. Salvation takes place sooner or later in a moment of time and human history, and the skilled teacher is the means towards that perfection. In the Western traditions the religious teacher who is cognizant of the present life as distinguished from afterlife, as two separate moments and conditions of life, does not face the same challenge or fall under the same necessity to be an extraordinary personality. But in India complete liberation and full human perfection are the goals of successful education. India has responded to this basic theological understanding in terms of human psychology which has in the course of centuries developed practical ways of instruction.

Tagore, Gandhi and Sri Aurobindo, in greater and lesser degree, grounded their educational thought and praxis in psychology. The *āśram* context out of which they worked was founded upon psychological stages of human development. Just as Hindu theological concepts are psychologically graded, so too educational theory is according to psychological levels of development. To educate, for Tagore, Gandhi and Sri Aurobindo, is to build a new psychology. And since they were educational pioneers, it was frequently the discovery of a new psychology. Because Indian education stands firmly within a psychological tradition, and this is true even with the innovations of Tagore, Gandhi and Sri Aurobindo, the personality of man becomes the principal medium of education. The role of the teacher is unique because the success of his instruction depends less upon his ideology or pedagogy than upon his personality. One could possibly observe other practical activities than education in the lives of Gandhi, Tagore and Sri Aurobindo, but in each case it will be discovered that the medium and source of their impact were their personalities. What they achieved as religious personalities effected all that they achieved in education. The achievement of personality was the achievement of truth. Education for them was the communication of the truth of the personality.

13. Betty Heimann, *Facets of Indian Thought*, p. 81.

Glossary

ācārya : a teacher who imparts a broad range of socio-religious knowledge.

ādeśa : an interior inspiration or command believed to come from the divine.

ahiṃsā : non-injury; non-violence; reconceptualized by Gandhi to include a quality of love and redemptive suffering.

ānanda-yoga : a spiritual path characterized as joyful and filled with aesthetic delight; the aesthetic path toward liberation.

anaśakti : non-attachment; self-less activity.

āsana-s : the physical postures in the practice of *hatha-yoga.*

āśram : a place for spiritual discipline and dvelopment within a communal setting.

avatār : one who in the course of history is regarded as a special descent (literally, a descender) from the region of liberation in order to renovate man and world.

Bhagavad Gītā : The Song of the Lord; a Hindu poem forming part of the epical *Mahābhārata* which teaches liberation by love and divine grace.

bhakti : devotion; love; a *bhaktin* is one devoted to the divine.

bhakti-yoga : the yoga or path of devotion toward liberation; a *bhakti-yogin* is one who follows the path of devotion as his primary spiritual discipline.

bhūma : fullness; completion.

brahmācārya : the first stage of life; the student years wherein during ancient times the student lived with his spiritual teacher and devoted himself to both secular and spiritual discipline; a time of celibacy.

Brahman : Divine Reality; Absolute Reality.

buddhi : a faculty of the mind designating a higher intelligence; although not the highest understanding, it is the faculty of illumination and wisdom.

cakras : seven centres (literally, wheels) of psycho-physical energy within the body.

citta : a faculty of the mind designating memory and recognition of the objects of the external world.

darśan : the sight of the *guru* which may initiate spiritual awakening.

dharma : moral duty; the moral and social law as the most fundamental norm of human conduct.

dhyāna : meditation.

dīkṣā : the grace of the *guru* communicated by touch, sight, word or through consciousness; an initiation by the *guru* which may transform the student.

durāgraha : bad-grasping; foolish obstinacy; for Gandhi, holding to predetermined goals.

guru : spiritual teacher, master.

guru-bhakti : devotion to the teacher.

gurukula : a residential hermitage for *guru* and disciples.

guru-śiṣya : the teacher-student relationship.

harṣa : an aesthetic term designating the joy sought in the artistic work itself.

hatha-yoga : the physical postures and physical discipline of *yoga*.

jīvātman : the individual self.

jñāna : knowledge; wisdom.

jñāna yoga : the path of knowledge; a *jñāna-yogin* is one who follows the path of knowledge as his primary spiritual discipline.

kāma : desire; as a goal of life designating the sensual, sensitive and aesthetic development of man.

karma : the law according to which every deed has its inevitable consequence, a good deed has a good consequence, and an evil deed an evil consequence; also work, activity.

karma-yoga : the path of activity; a *karma-yogin* is one who follows the path of activity as his primary spiritual discipline.

kīrtans : communal celebrations of devotional song and prayer.

līlā : the cosmic play or dance of the divine.

Mahābhārata : one of the two great religious epics of Hinduism (3rd—2nd cent. BCE) ascribed to the legendary Vyāsa; for centuries a source of popular entertainment, religious and moral instruction.

manas : a faculty of the mind designating the logical and reasoning function.

mantra : a verse, word or syllable from the Vedas considered sacred, recited for its effect in meditation, usually given an esoteric interpretation.

māyā : ephemeral or phenomenal reality; the veil (illusion) hiding ultimate reality from man's ego.

mokṣa : freedom from earthly bondage; liberation, salvation.

Nai Talim : a national programme of basic education advanced by Gandhi.

paramātman : the universal self.

prāṇayama (*prāṇāyāma*) : the discipline of ordered breathing in *yoga*.

Purāṇas : Indian religious literature of a legendary and mythological character.

purṇa-yoga : integral *yoga* as advanced by Sri Aurobindo.

purohita : a teacher who performs priestly functions.

puruṣārthas : the four traditional goals of Hindu life.

rāja-yoga : the discipline of meditation, that is, a mastery of the activities of the mind.

Rāmāyaṇa : one of the two great religious epics of Hinduism (1st cent. BCE) ascribed to the sage Vālmīki; shorter and more homogeneous than the *Mahābhārata*, its hero Rāma came to be accepted as an *avatār* of Viṣṇu; numerous vernacular versions developed in South Asia.

rasa : taste, flavour; the aesthetic sense or an aesthetic quality.

ṛṣi : traditionally a Vedic sage or seer; frequently applied honorifically to figures exhibiting special insight into divine reality.

ṛta : a universal principle; the unchanging law, physical and moral, real and eternal, upon which the whole universe is founded.

Sachidānanda : the Divine Existence, Consciousness and Bliss.

sādhaks : spiritual seekers within an *āśram* community.

sādhana : a spirituality; the undertaking of a religious discipline.

sādhu : a general term for an Indian holy man, ranging from the ascetic to the wonder-worker.

sahitya : Sanskrit word for literature; literally, that which binds.

śakti : the creative power of the divine; conceived as female and mythically represented in the consorts of the gods; plays a significant role in Tantrism.

saṃskāras : traditional Hindu religious ceremonies; sacraments.

sant : a word now used generally to designate a popular religious figure; a saint.

sarvodaya : literally, the uplift of all; name given by Gandhi to social and moral renovation.

śāstras : Sanskrit for command, book; name given to a sacred book or manual of religious teaching.

sattva : one of three qualities of the phenomenal world; characterized as intelligence, orderliness, harmonious relationship.

satya : truth, the real.

satyāgraha : holding to truth, truth-grasping; a truth-force, a soul-force; the path followed and the technique developed by Gandhi for change based on truth, *ahiṃsā*, and redemptive suffering; a *satyāgrahi* refers to a member of Gandhi's non-violent campaign.

svadharma : one's own *dharma* (moral law, moral duty).

swadeshi : of indigenous or native make; the principle of using goods made locally or in one's own country.

swarāj : self-rule; home-rule; used in the independence movement from Tilak to Gandhi.

tamas : one of the three qualities of the phenomenal world, characterized as darkness, inertia, the veiling power of *māyā*.

tapasya : a spiritual discipline, possibly a penitential discipline.

tapovanas : an ancient forest community for youth and their teachers.

upādhyāya : a teacher who imparts only the sacred Vedas.

upanayana : the ceremony of initiation (literally, drawing near) in which the Hindu youth is 'twice born' and attains full membership in one of the three higher castes; sacred thread ceremony.

Upaniṣads : sacred Sanskrit texts, the last of the Vedas, expressing a highly spiritual and philosophical experience of divine reality (800-400 BCE); revelation (*śruti*).

Vedas : literally, knowledge ; general term for the sacred Sanskrit texts of early Brahmanical Hinduism; revelation (*śruti*); includes hymns, rituals, expository and meditational literature.

yoga : literally, uniting, yoking or harnessing one's mental and physical powers; most typically refers to self-discipline and meditation; most generally refers to the path or discipline of spirituality, for example, devotion, activity, knowledge; one who undertakes such a discipline is a *yogi*.

Bibliography

Ashby, Philip H., *Modern Trends in Hinduism* (New York: Columbia University Press, 1974),

Ashe, Geoffrey, *Gandhi* (New York : Stein & Day, 1968).

Avinashlingam, T.S., *Educational Philosophy of Swami Vivekananda* (Coimbatore: Sri Ramakrishna Vidyalaya, 1964).

———com., *Education—Swami Vivekananda* (Coimbtore: Sri Ramakrishna Vidyalaya, 1958).

———and K. Swaminathan, *World Teachers on Education* (Coimbatore: Sri Ramakrishna Vidyalaya, 1958).

Bhattacharya, Rinibas, *Tagore and the World* (Calcutta: Dasgupta and Co., 1961).

Bondurant, Joan V., *Conquest of Violence, The Gandhian Philosophy of Conduct* (Berkeley: University of California Press, rev. edit., 1965).

Bose, Buddhadeva, *Tagore: Portrait of a Poet* (Bombay: University of Bombay, 1962).

Cenkner, William, "Gandhi and Creative Conflict," *Thought*, Vol. XLV, No. 178, Autumn 1970.

———"Gandhi's Ahimsa : The Transformation of an Ethical Value," *That They May Live*, edit. George Devine (New York: Alba House, 1972).

———"Religion and Education: Models from Contemporary Hinduism," *Religious Education*, Vol. LXX, No. 4 July-Aug., 1975.

———"Tagore and Aesthetic Man," *International Philosophical Quarterly*. Vol. XIII, No. 2, June 1973.

Cenkner William, "Tagore's Vision of Relationality," *Humanitas*, Vol. XII No. I, February 1975.

Chaitanya, Krishna, *A New History of Sanskrit Literature* (Bombay : Asia Publishing House, 1962).

Chakravarty, Amiya, ed. *A Tagore Reader* (Boston : Beacon Press, 1961).

Chaturvedi, *Tagore at Shantiniketan, A Survey of Rabindranath Tagore's Educational Experiments at Shantiniketan* (Bombay: Mathai's Publications, 1934).

Chaudhuri, Haridas & Frederic Spiegelberg, *The Integral Philosophy of Sri Aurobindo* (London: Geoge Allen & Unwin, 1960).

Chethimattam, John Britto, "Rasa, The Soul of Indian Art," *International Philosophical Quarterly*, Vol. X, No. 1, 1970.

Calaco, Paul, *The Absolute in the Philosophy of Aurobindo Ghose* (Rome: Pontificia Universitas Gregoriana, 1954).

Dasgupta, Manoj, "Experience of a Student-Professor of the Sri Aurobindo International Centre of Education," *Sri Aurobindo Circle*, 20, 1964.

Datta, Dhirendra Mohan, *The Philosophy of Mahatma Gandhi* (Madison: University of Wisconsin, 1953).

Diwakar, R. R., *Mahayogi Sri Aurobindo* (Bombay: Bharatiya Vidya Bhavan, 1967).

Dowsett, Norman C., "Change of Climate in the United Nations Organization," *Mother India*, Vol. XXII, No. 2, March 1970.

Elder, Joseph W., "The Gandhian Ethic of Work in India," *Religious Ferment in Asia*, edit., Robert J. Miller (Wichita: University of Kansas, 1974).

Fischer, Louis, *The Life of Mahatma Gandhi* (New York: Harper & Bros., 1951).

Gandhi, M. K., *An Autobiography, The Story of My Experiments with Truth*, trans. Mahadev Desai (Boston: Beacon Press, 1956).

———*Ashram Observances in Action*, trans., Valji G. Desai Ahmedabad: Navajivan Press, 1955).

———*Basic Education* (Ahmedabad: Navajivan Press, 1951).

———*Educational Reconstruction* (Wardha: Hindustani Talimi Sangh, 1939).

Gandhi, M. K., *From Yervada Mandir*, trans., Valji G. Desai (Ahmedabad : Navajivan Press, 3rd edit., 1945).

———*Gandhiji's Thoughts on Education*, comp. T. S. Avinashlingam (New Delhi: Ministry of Education, 1958).

———*Gita-My Mother*, edit., Anand T. Hingorani (Bombay: Bharatiya Vidya Bhavan, 1965).

———*Hindu Dharma* (Ahmedabad: Navajivan Publishing House, 1950).

———*In Search of the Supreme*, edit., V.B. Kher (Ahmedabad: Navajivan Press, 1961).

——— *Message to Students*, edit., A. T. Hingorani (Allahabad: Leader Press, 1958).

———*My Views on Education*, edit., A.T. Hingorani (Bombay: Bharatiya Vidya Bhavan, 1951).

———*Non-Violence in Peace and War*, edit., Bharatan Kumarappa (Ahmedabad: Navajivan Press, 1942).

———*Non-Violence Resistance* (New York: Schocken Books, 1961).

———*Satyagraha, Non-Violent Resistance*, edit., Bharatan Kumarappa (Ahmedabad: Navajivan Press, 1951).

———*Speeches and Writings of Mahatma Gandhi* (Madras: Natesan, 4th edit., n.d.).

———*The Collected Works of Mahatma Gandhi* (New Delhi: The Publications Division).

———*The Mind of Mahatma Gandhi*, comp. R.K. Prabhu & U. R. Rao (Ahmedabad: Navajivan Press, 1945).

———*The Problem of Education* (Ahmedabad: Navajivan Publishing House, 1962).

———*The Task Before Students*, comp., R.K. Prabhu (Ahmedabad: Navajivan Publishing House, 1961).

———*To the Students* (Ahmedabad: Navajivan Publishing House, 1949).

———*True Education* (Ahmedabad: Navajivan Publishing House, 1962).

Ghose, Sisirkumar, "Total Education," *Mother India*, Vol. XVIII, No. 7, August 1966.

Ghose, Sookamal, edit., *The Century Book of Tagore* (Calcutta: Granthan, Prakash Chandra Saha, 1961).

Gupta, Nolini Kanta, *Sri Aurobindo and His Ashram* (Pondicherry: Sri Aurobindo Ashram, 1948).

———(Gupta, Nolini Kanta) & K. Amrita, *Reminiscences* (Pondicherry: Sri Aurobindo Ashram, 1969).

Hay, Stephen N., *Asian Ideas of East and West* (Boston: Harvard University Press, 1970).

Heimann, Betty, *Facets of Indian Thought* (London: George Allen & Unwin, Ltd., 1964).

Horsburgh, H.J.H., *Non-Violence and Aggression, A Study of Gandhi's Moral Equivalent of War* (London: Oxford University Press, 1968).

Husain, Zakir, *Education in the World of Tomorrow* (Bombay: The Progressive Group, 1945).

Iyengar, K.R. Srinivas, *Sri Aurobindo: A Biography and a History* (Pondichery: Sri Aurobindo Ashram, 3rd rev. edit., 1972).

———*Sri Aurobindo: An Introduction* (Mysore: Rao & Raghvan, 1961).

Joshi, Kireet M., "Sri Aurobindo Ashram as an International Institution of Research in Education and Yoga," *The Advent*, Vol. XXIV, No. 2, April 1967.

Kabir, Humayun, *Education in New India* (London: George Allen & Unwin, Ltd., 1956).

———*Indian Philosophy of Education* (Bombay: Asia Publishing House, 1961).

Kripalani, J.B., *The Latest Fad, Basic Education* (Sevagram, Wardha: Hindustani Talimi Sangh, 1948).

Kripalani, Krishna, *Tagore: A Life* (New Delhi: Malancha, 1961).

LeCocq, Rhoda P., *The Radical Thinkers, Heidegger and Sri Aurobindo* (Pondicherry: Sri Aurobindo Ashram, 1969).

Lesny, V., *Rabindranath Tagore, His Personality and Work*, trans., Guy McKeever Phillips (London: George Allen & Unwin, Ltd., 1939).

Maitra, S.K., *An Introduction to the Philosophy of Sri Aurobindo* (Benares: Benares Hindu University, 1941).

Mathur, Vishwanath Sahai, edit, *Gandhiji as an Educationist, A Symposium* (Delhi: Metropolitan Book Co., Ltd., 1951).

McDermott, Robert, edit., *The Essential Aurobindo* (New York: Schocken Books, 1973).

Miri, Indira, *Mahatma Gandhi's Educational Theory* (New Delhi: Gandhian Thought, n.d.).

Misra, Ram Shankar, *The Integral Advaitism of Sri Aurobindo* (Benares: Benares Hindu University, 1957).

Mitra, Sisirkumar, *The Liberator : Sri Aurobindo, India and the World* (Bombay : Jaico Publishing House, 1970).

Mohanty, Jitendranath, "Modern Philosophical Anthropology," *Sri Aurobindo Circle*, No. 12, 1956.

Mookerjee, Reena, "Gandhi and Tagore: On Man," *Gandhi Centenary Volume* (Santiniketan: Visva-Bharati University, 1969).

Mother India, Special Issuse for the Silver Jubilee of the Sri Aurobindo International Centre of Education, Vol. XX, No. 10-11, Nov.-Dec. 1968.

Mukherjee, H.B., *Education for Fulness: A Study of the Educational Thought and Experiment of Rabindranath Tagore* (Bompay : Asia Publishing House, 1962).

Naravane, V.S., *Modern Indian Thought* (Bombay: Asia Publishing House, 1964).

——— *Rabindranath Tagore: A Philosophical Study* (Allahabad: Central Book Depot, 1946).

Narayan, Shriman, *Towards Better Education* (Ahmedabad; Navajivan Publishing House, 1969).

Nehru, Jawaharlal, *Mahatma Gandhi* (Bombay & New York: Asia Publishing House, 1965).

———*Nehru on Gandhi* (New York; Signet Press, n.d.).

Nirodbaran, *Talks with Sri Aurobindo* (Pondicherry: Sri Aurobindo Ashram, 1966).

Pandit, Madhav P., *Handbook, Sri Aurobindo University Centre* (Pondicherry: Sri Aurobindo Ashram, 1968).

———*Reminiscences and Anecdotes of Sri Aurobindo* (Pondicherry: Sri Aurobindo Ashram, 1966).

Panter-Brick, Simone, *Gandhi Against Machiavellism, Non-Violence in Politics* (London : Asia Publishing House, 1966).

Patel, M.S., *The Educational Philosophy of Mahatma Gandhi* (Ahmedabad: Navajivan Press, 1953).

Pearson, Nathaniel, *Sri Aurobindo and the Soul Quest of Man* (London: George Allen & Unwin, Ltd., 1952).

Pillai, N.P., *The Educational Aims of Mahatma Gandhi* (Trivandrum: Kalyanmandir Publications, 1959).

Prasad, Narayan, *Life in Sri Aurobindo Ashram* (Pondicherry: Sri Aurobindo Ashram, 1968).

Purani, A.B., *Sri Aurobindo's Life Divine* (Pondicherry: Sri Aurobindo Ashram, 1966).

——— *The Life of Sri Aurobindo* (Pondicherry: Sri Aurobindo Ashram, 2nd edit., 1960).

Pyarelal, Nair, *Mahatma Gandhi: The Last Phase* (Ahmedabad: Navajivan Press, 1956-58).

Radhakrishnan, S. & J. H. Muirhead, *Contemporary Indian Phliosophy* (New York: Macmillan Co., 1936).

Ramachandran & Mahadevan, editors, *Gandhi: His Relevance for Our Times* (New Delhi: Gandhi Peace Foundation, 1967).

Ramanathan, G., *Education from Dewey to Gandhi* (Bombay: Asia Publishing House, 1962).

Ramji, Marni Tata, *The Concept of Personality in the Educational Thought of Mahatma Gandhi* (New Delhi: National Council of Educational Research & Training, 1969).

Rawson, Philip, *Indian Sculpture* (New York: E. P. Dutton & Co., 1962).

Ray, Sibnarayan, edit., *Gandhi, India and the World, An International Symposium* (Bombay: Nachiketa Publications, Ltd., 1970).

Rothermund, Indira, *The Philosophy of Restraint* (Bombay: Popular Prakashan, 1963).

Roy, Anilbaran, edit., *The Message of the Gita as Interpreted by Sri Aurobindo* (London: George Allen & Unwin, Ltd., 1946).

Roy, Dilip Kumar, *Sri Aurobindo Came to me* (Bombay: Jaico Publishing House, 1964).

Saint-Hilaire, P. B. (Pavitra), *Education and the Aim of Human Life* (Pondicherry: Sri Aurobindo International Centre of Education, 1967).

——— *The Message of Sri Aurobindo and His Ashram* (Pondicherry: Sri Aurobindo Ashram, 1947).

Saiyidain, K.G., *The Humanist Tradition in Indian Educational Thought* (London: Asia Publishing House, 1966).

Sarkar, Sunil Chandra. *Tagore's Educational Philosophy and Experiment* (Santiniketan : Visva-Bharati, 1961).

Satprem, *Sri Aurobindo: Or The Adventure of Consciousness*, trans. Tehmi (Pondicherry: Sri Aurobindo Ashram, 1968).

Seminar on Educational Reconstruction: Report (Bombay: Gandhi Smarak Nidhi, 1963).

Sen Gupta, Santosh Chandra, edit., *Rabindranath Tagore: Homage from Visva-Bharati,* (Santiniketan: Visva-Bharati, 1962).

Sen, Indra, "Visit of the Education Commission to Pondicherry," *Mother India*, Vol. XVII, No. 10-11, Nov.-Dec., 1965.

Shrimali, K. L., *The Wardha Scheme, The Gandhian Plan of Education for Rural India* (Udaipur: Vidya Bhawan Society, 1949).

Sinha, Sasadhar, *Social Thinking of Rabindranath Tagore* (Bombay: Asia Publishing House, 1962).

Sri Aurobindo, *A Scheme of Education*, edit., Pranab K. Bhattacharya (Pondicherry: Sri Aurobindo Asharam, n.d.).

——— *Correspondence with Sri Aurobindo*, comp., Nirodbaran (Pondicherry: Sri Aurobindo Ashram, 1969).

———*Integral Education*, comp., Indra Sen (Pondicherry: Sri Aurobindo International University Centre, 1952).

———*Lights on Yoga* (Pondicherry: Sri Aurobindo Ashram, 1942).

———*On Yoga I, The Synthesis of Yoga* (Pondicherry: Sri Aurobindo Ashram, 1969).

———*On Yoga II* (Pondicherry: Sri Aurobindo Ashram, 1958).

———*Speeches* (Pondicherry: Sri Aurobindo Ashram, 3rd edit., 1952).

———*Sri Aurobindo on Himself*, Vol. XXVI, Sri Aurobindo Birth Centenary Library (Pondicherry: Sri Aurobindo Ashram, 1972).

———*Sri Aurobindo on Himself and on The Mother* (Pondicherry: Sri Aurobindo Ashram, 1958).

———*The Brain af India* (Pondicherry: Sri Aurobindo Ashram, 1967).

———*The Destiny of Man* (Pondicherry: Sri Aurobindo Ashram, 1969).

———*The Human Cycle* (Pondicherry: Sri Aurobindo Ashram, 1962).

———*The Ideal of Human Unity*, abrid. Sisirkumar Ghose (Calcutta: Sri Aurobindo Pathamandir, 1972).

Sri Aurobindo, *The Life Divine* (Pondicherry: Sri Aurobindo Ashram, 2nd imp., 1960).

Sri Aurobindo & The Mother, *Integral Education: In the Words of Sri Aurobindo and The Mother*, comp. Indra Sen (Pondicherry: Sri Aurobindo International University Centre, 1952).

———*Sri Aurobindo & The Mother on Education* (Pondicherry: Sri Aurobindo Ashram, 1956).

———*Sri Aurobindo & The Mother on Education*, Part I, II, III (Pondicherry: Sri Aurobindo Society, 1972).

———*Sri Aurobindo & The Mother on Physical Education* (Pondicherry: Sri Aurobindo Ashram, 1967).

Sri Aurobindo Birth Centenary Library (Pondicherry: Sri Aurobindo Ashram, 1972).

Vol. 15, *Social and Political Thought*.

Vol. 16, *The Supramental Manifestation*.

Vol. 18 & 19, *The Life Divine*.

Vol. 20 & 21, *The Synthesis of Yoga*.

Vol. 22, 23 & 24, *Letters on Yoga*.

Srivastava, Rama Shanker, *Contemporary Indian Philosophy* (Delhi: Munshiram Manoharlal, 1965).

Suryanarayana, A.V. , *Tagore as Educationist* (Madras: M.S.R. Murty & Co., 1962).

Sykes, Marjorie, *Rabindranath Tagore* (London : Longmans, Green & Co. , Ltd., 1943).

Tagore, Rabindranath, *A Flight of Swans, Poems from Balaka* (London: John Murray, 2nd edit., 1962).

———"A Poet's School," *Visva Bharati Quarterly*, Vol. IV, No. 3, Oct. 1962.

———*Ashrama Education* (Santiniketan: Visva-Bharati, n.d.).

———*Creative Unity* (London: Macmillan & Co., Ltd., Indian Edition, 1962).

———"Education for Rural India," *Visva Bharati Quarterly*, Education Number, Vol. XIII, May-Oct. 1947.

——— *Gitanjali*, trans. by author (London: Macmillan & Co., Ltd. Indian Edition, 1966).

———*Lectures* and *Addresses*, edit. Anthony X. Soares (London: Macmillan & Co., Ltd., 1928).

———*Letters from Abroad* (Madras: S. Ganesan, 1924).

Tagore, Rabindranath, *Letters to a Friend*, edit. C.F. Andrews (New York: Macmillan Co., 1929).

———*Lipika* (Bomay: Jaico Publishing House, 1969).

———*My Boyhood Days*, trans. Marjorie Sykes (Calcutta: Visva-Bharati, 1940).

———*My Reminiscences* (London: Macmillan & Co., Ltd., 1917).

———*Personality* (London : Macmillan & Co., Ltd., 1965).

———"Rabindranath Tagore in Russia," *Visva-Bharati Bulletin*, No.1 5, Nov. 1930.

———*Sadhana* (London: Macmillan & Co., Ltd., Indian Edition, 1965).

———*Sri Aurobindo and Rabindranath Tagore* (Pondicherry: Sri Aurobindo Ashram, 1961).

———"Sriniketan, "*Visva-Bharati News*, Vol. VII, No. 8, Feb. 1939.

———*The Housewarming and Other Selected Writings*, trans. Mary Lago, Tarun Gupta and Amiya Chakravarty (New York: New American Library, 1965).

———"The Place of Music in Education and Culture," *Visva-Bharati Quarterly*, Education Number, Vol. VIII, May-Oct. 1947.

———"The Relation of the Universe and the Individual," *The Modern Review*, Vol. XIV, No. 1, July 1913.

———*The Religion of Man* (Boston: Beacon Press, 1961).

———"The Schoolmaster," *The Modern Review*, Vol. XXVI, No. 4, May 1924.

———The Union of Cultures," *The Modern Review*, Vol. XXX, No. 5, Nov. 1921.

———*Thoughts from Rabindranath Tagore* (London: MacMillan & Co., Ltd., 1933).

———"Thoughts on Education", *Visva-Bharati Quarterly*, Education Number, Vol. XIII, May-Oct. 1947.

———"To the Child", *The Modern Review*, Vol. XXXVII, No. 5, May, 1925.

———*Towards Universal Man* (London: Asia Publishing House, 1961).

———*Wings of Death*, trans. Aurobindo Bose (London: John Murray, 1960).

Tagore, R. & Leonard K. Elmhirst, *Rabindranath Tagore: Pioneer in Education* (London : John Murray, 1961).

Tendulkar, Dinanath Gopal, *Mahatma: Life of M. K. Gandhi* (Bombay: Jhaveri & Tendulkar, 1951-54).

The Mother, *Conversations* (Pondicherry: Sri Aurobindo Ashram, 1966).

———*On India: Some Problems and Solutions* (Pondicherry: Sri Aurobindo Ashram, 1970).

———*The Mother on Sri Aurobindo* (Pondicherry: Sri Aurobindo Ashram, 1961).

———*Words of the Mother* (Pondicherry: Sri Aurobindo, Ashram 3rd Series, 1946).

Thompson, Edwards, *Rabindranath Tagore: Poet and Dramatist* (London: Oxford University Press, 2nd edit., 1948).

Verma, I.B., *Basic Education: A Reinterpretation* (Agra: Sri Ram Mehra & Co., 1969).

Index